MASTERPIECES

With a new bibliography
by Adolf K. Placzek

OF FURNITURE

IN PHOTOGRAPHS AND

MEASURED DRAWINGS

VERNA COOK SALOMONSKY

THIRD EDITION

DOVER PUBLICATIONS, INC./ NEW YORK

Published in Canada by General Publishing Company, Ltd., 30 Lesmill Road, Don Mills, Toronto, Ontario.

Published in the United Kingdom by Constable and Company, Ltd., 10 Orange Street, London WC 2.

This Dover edition, first published in 1953, is a revised edition of the work originally published by the Periodical Publishing Company, Grand Rapids, Michigan, in 1931 under the title *Masterpieces of Furniture Design*.

The third edition, first published by Dover in 1974, contains a new Preface.

We are grateful to the following museums for their kind assistance and permission to reproduce the photographs used in this book: Metropolitan Museum of Art, Boston Museum of Fine Arts, Rhode Island School of Design, Essex Institute, Hispanic Society of America.

International Standard Book Number: 0-486-21381-1
Library of Congress Catalog Card Number: 53-8384

Manufactured in the United States of America
Dover Publications, Inc.
180 Varick Street
New York, N. Y. 10014

FOREWORD

THE object of this collection of plates, made available through the courtesy of the museums previously mentioned, is to give furniture designers, decorators, students, collectors and all others interested in fine furniture, a more comprehensive knowledge of representative pieces of furniture, executed in former centuries.

The pieces selected were made during the sixteenth, seventeenth, eighteenth and early years of the nineteenth centuries in the countries most advanced in the art of cabinet making.

In choosing the specimens of furniture studied, an effort has been made to select subjects that will serve best, both as sources of inspiration for original designs, and as models for the manufacture of replicas.

In order that the reader may better understand the traditions and influences governing the form and character of these designs a short explanatory text accompanies each plate. A photograph of the piece is also included, to supply information which the line drawings are not competent to convey.

Verna Cook Salomonsky

New York, December, 1930.

PREFACE TO THE THIRD (1974) EDITION

Scholarship in the evaluation of furniture has made great advances in recent years. Attribution and dating by experts have become far more precise and accurate than they were formerly. It is not surprising, therefore, that some of the information in the 1953 edition of this book has been revealed as incorrect by recent work in the field. Changes in possession, as well as changes of fact as reflected by current scholarship, are listed below, according to plate number.

2. This piece is no longer in the collection of the Brooklyn Museum.
3. The chair dates from the first half of the seventeenth century.
5. The chair is now described as being in the style of Charles II.
6. The chair, no longer in the collection of the Metropolitan Museum of Art, is dated as c. 1690.
7. The chair is no longer in the collection of the Metropolitan Museum of Art.
8. The chair, which is actually of maple, is now identified as American, 1700–1725, and is not in the style of Charles II.
9. The piece is now described as a couch or daybed.
11. The chair dates from 1650–1700.
12. The arm chairs are American.
13. Ash is used in the upper side stretchers.
14. The arm chair, now dated as 1715–1720, is in the early Georgian style.
15. The piece is now described as an early Georgian sofa.
19. The piece is now described as a daybed (lit de repos), and is dated as 1750–1775.
25. The sofa is English.
27. The chair is English.
29. This piece, no longer in the collection of the Metropolitan Museum of Art, dates from 1780–1790.
30. The piece, no longer in the collection of the Metropolitan Museum of Art, is called a daybed in the style of the Adam Brothers, and dates from 1780–1790.
31. This chair is now dated as c. 1800.
32. This chair is now dated as c. 1800.
33. This chair is now dated as c. 1800.

35. The piece is no longer in the collection of the Metropolitan Museum of Art.
37. The chairs are in the style of Duncan Phyfe.
38. The chair is in the style of Duncan Phyfe.
44. The table is dated as c. 1700.
45. The table is dated as c. 1700.
46. The table is dated as c. 1725.
51. The piece is no longer in the collection of the Metropolitan Museum of Art.
52. The card table is now dated as 1770–1780.
56. The table is English.
57. The table is now dated as early nineteenth century.
58. The table is now described as a card table, dating from c. 1800.
60. The piece is no longer in the collection of the Metropolitan Museum of Art.
62. The table is no longer attributed to Duncan Phyfe.
67. The table is definitely from Baltimore.
68. The chest dates from the first half of the sixteenth century.
69. The cupboard dates from the late fifteenth century.
71. The piece is now described as a chest with three drawers.
72. The piece is American, and dates from 1755–1795.
74. The piece has birch verneer rather than satinwood inlay.
75. The commode is American.
78. The piece is no longer in the collection of the Metropolitan Museum of Art.
83. The piece is of mahogany and satinwood.
84. The piece dates from the seventeenth century.
85. The piece, no longer in the collection of the Metropolitan Museum of Art, dates from the early eighteenth century.
87. The secretary is no longer attributed to John Goddard, and dates from 1760–1775.
88. The piece is no longer in the collection of the Metropolitan Museum of Art.
89. The secretary was built by William Appleton.
90. The piece is no longer in the collection of the Metropolitan Museum of Art.
91. The piece is dated as 1700–1720.
93. The piece is dated as 1740–1775.
98. The dressing glass is American.
99. The mirrors are no longer in the collection of the Metropolitan Museum of Art.

LIST OF PLATES

CHAIRS AND SETTEES

PLATES

SIDE CHAIR
Italian XVI Century

THE creative ability of the Italians during the 16th century is reflected in the designing and fashioning of furniture, as well as in the other arts. England and France received much inspiration from this period of the Italian Renaissance.

The dominant characteristics of this furniture were a strongly developed architectural character of outline, the absence of luxurious comfort which we find in many of the succeeding styles, and the feeling of dignity attained by well balanced construction and richly ornamented surfaces, contrasting with structural frames of simple designs.

The contour of this piece is characteristic of 16th century Italian chairs. The deeply tenoned stretchers and rails give a decided staunchness to its structure.

A point of difference between this and other models lies in the broad stretcher between the fore legs which is decoratively scrolled and pierced. In addition, the underpart of the side stretchers are shaped.

The unpadded back and the padded seat are covered with leather and held in place by rows of brass headed nails. The intricate design on the back leather is exquisitely tooled in gold.

The acanthus finials, terminating the back supports, are typical of this period. In this instance, they are gilded and it is quite probable that this gilding has been applied over a coat of red, superimposed on a coat of white.

The short fringe around the lower edge of the seat apron and at the bottom of the back is of dull green silk.

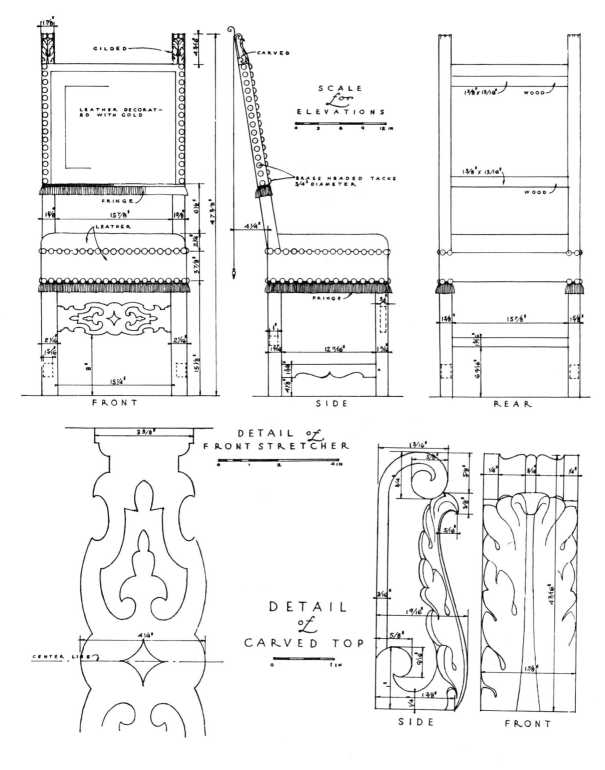

SIDE CHAIR
Italian XVI century (Walnut)
NOW IN THE METROPOLITAN MUSEUM OF ART

ITALIAN ARM CHAIR
XVI Century

THE interiors of Italian palaces in the early Renaissance were graced by but few pieces of furniture. Chests, benches, stools and chairs, beds and tables were usually considered all that was necessary. Walnut was the wood most generally used.

This particular chair was built in the 16th century, the period of the "High Renaissance." Craftsmen at that time knew the efficient use and combination of materials. They were fully aware of the effect to be obtained by relieving the severity of line with the introduction of rich carvings, turnings or patterns of cut-out design. Their ability in this direction is illustrated in this chair by the bold scrolled outline at the lower edge of the broad front stretcher.

Thick leather, tacked to the back posts, is without support except by one cross rail at the top of the back. The leather forming the seat is attached only to the side rails and is tacked to the four leg members. The seat is without framework at front and rear.

The arms are perfectly horizontal with broadening tops which return sharply at their juncture with the back posts. This projection at the top of the arms rolls over at the front.

An optical illusion is produced by the photograph which gives the legs the appearance of slanting toward the top, whereas in reality all of the legs are perpendicular.

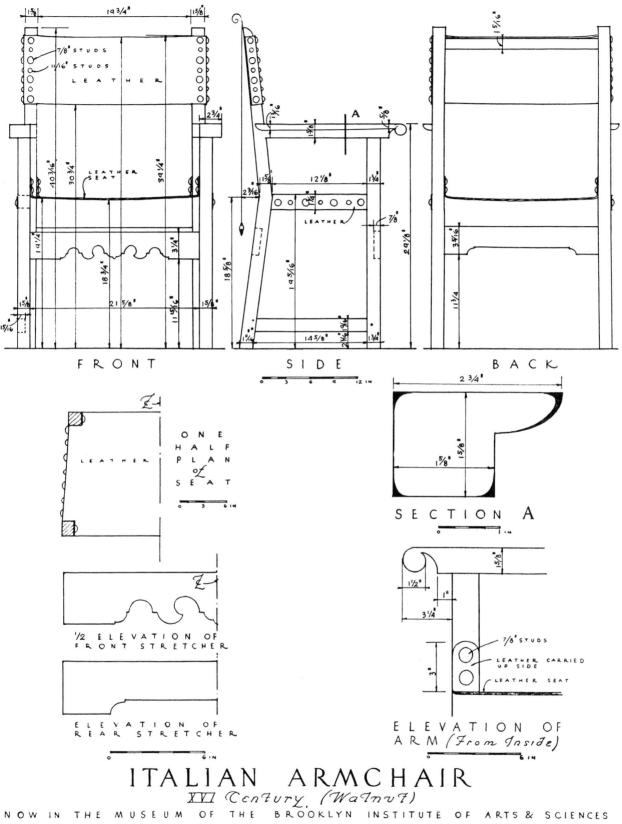

ITALIAN ARMCHAIR
XVI Century (Walnut)
N O W   I N   T H E   M U S E U M   O F   T H E   B R O O K L Y N   I N S T I T U T E   O F   A R T S & S C I E N C E S

ITALIAN XVI CENTURY CHAIR

THE furniture of the Italian Renaissance did not attain the degree of luxury nor comfort which was so marked in both France and England.

This small side chair—presumably made for a child—is rectangular in form with the back slightly raked, the slant commencing at the seat line. The front legs, of delicate turning, rise above the level of the seat but are not covered by the upholstery. The uprights of the back, terminating in exceedingly delicate finials, are connected by upper and lower horizontal rails shaped in a scrolled pattern, strongly influenced by the Baroque. Large decorative rosettes are carved in the center of both the cresting and lower rail, which are joined by short, delicately turned spindles.

The seat, which tapers slightly toward the back, is covered with velvet brocade of a rich, red color, and finished at the lower edge with a narrow fringe of the same color. Small, turned buttons, recalling the designs of the larger rosettes on the back rails, conceal the heads of the wooden pegs on the legs and back supports.

The small side chairs were the most pleasing and the most successfully designed chairs of this time in Italy.

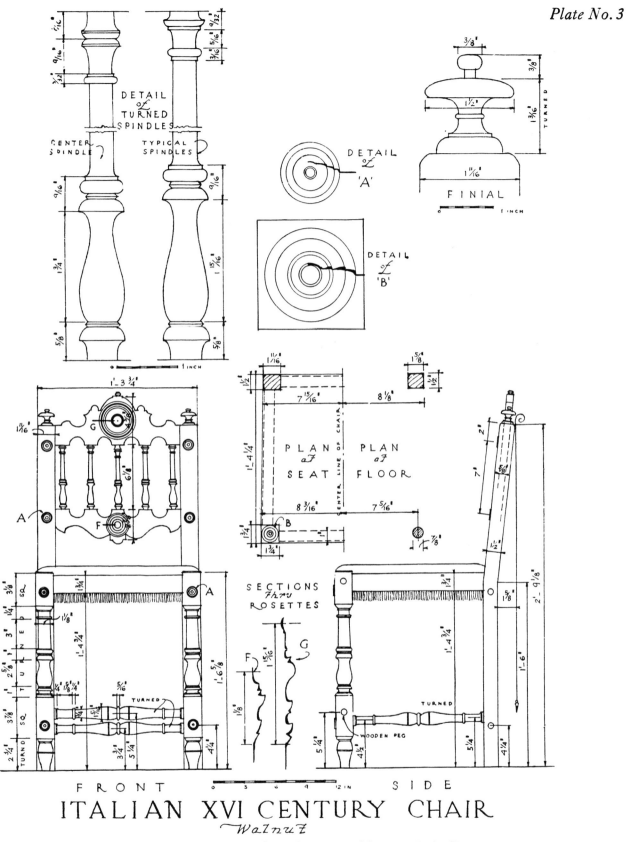

DETAIL of TURNED SPINDLES

CENTER SPINDLE

TYPICAL SPINDLES

DETAIL of 'A'

DETAIL of 'B'

FINIAL

PLAN of SEAT

PLAN of FLOOR

CENTER LINE OF CHAIR

SECTIONS thru ROSETTES

TURNED

WOODEN PEG

TURNED

FRONT

SIDE

ITALIAN XVI CENTURY CHAIR
Walnut
NOW IN THE METROPOLITAN MUSEUM OF ART

SPANISH CHAIR
XVII Century

THE few items of Spanish furniture which were in common use during the 17th century were those dictated by necessity. Of importance were chairs which in structural form resembled those of Italian origin. They were prevailingly rectilinear and of robust contour. Walnut was the material most frequently employed, although pine, oak and other woods were used to a lesser extent.

In the specimen shown here, knob and baluster-like turnings decorate the rectangular framework of back and leg supports. The contour of the rear legs, however, differs both in form and scale from that of the front legs. Of particular interest is the oddly shaped front stretcher, carved in bold relief.

The Spanish were excellent leather craftsmen, their products creating admiration throughout Europe. At this time, as well as in the 18th century, decorative leathers were used in Spain by cabinet makers for the coverings of seats and backs of chairs. These were held in place by rows of large brass-headed tacks, producing an ornamental edging at chair rails and at back supports. In this example a flowing Renaissance design is embossed upon the broad leather surfaces.

Also distinctly Spanish is the use of brass finials which in this chair are placed at the top of the back supports.

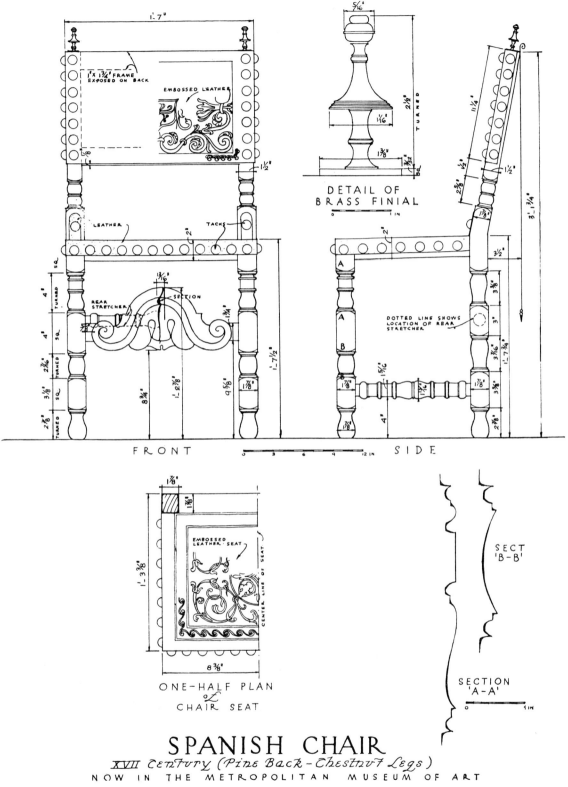

FRONT

SIDE

DETAIL OF
BRASS FINIAL

ONE-HALF PLAN
of
CHAIR SEAT

SECT
'B-B'

SECTION
'A-A'

SPANISH CHAIR
XVII Century (Pine Back - Chestnut Legs)
NOW IN THE METROPOLITAN MUSEUM OF ART

CROMWELLIAN TYPE ARM CHAIR
English About 1660

AFTER the reign of Charles I of England, the so-called Cromwellian style came into vogue, following on the heels of the Jacobean. The chairs of this period, made of hard wood, were of rather heavy character, although lighter than those of the previous style, with a square half-back and seat upholstered in leather of an Oriental fabric. An invariable feature of these chairs was the turned or twisted legs and stretchers, which made their appearance at this time and persisted for several centuries afterwards.

This particular arm-chair is made of walnut. The twisting and turnings are both easy and graceful. The square ends of the arms terminate in turned rosettes of excellent design.

The quaint charm, due in some measure to the squareness and sturdiness of its proportions, is heightened by an unusually attractive upholstery of petit point, with a design of bright flowers in tones of yellow on a blue-green field. This material, however, is undoubtedly of later date than the chair. The upholstery on the back is not cushioned but stretched and tacked to a heavy framework, exposed from the rear.

Side chairs of this style employ the same design.

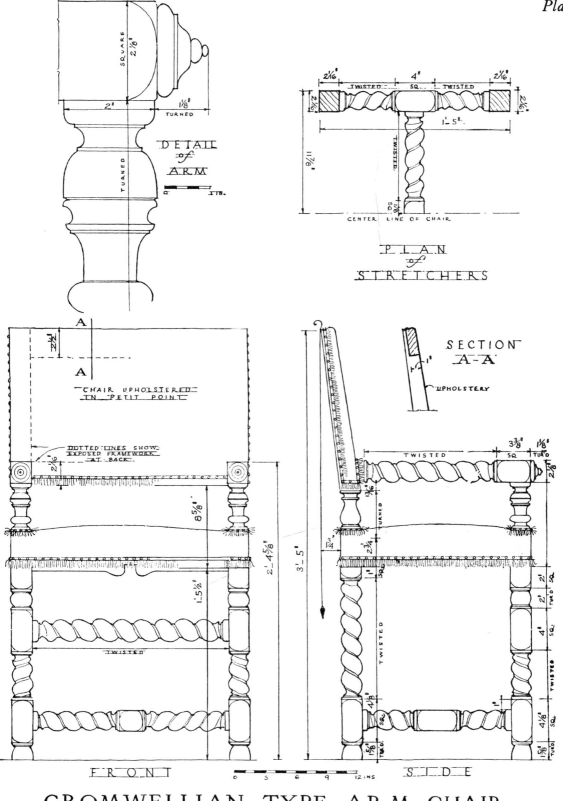

DETAIL
of
ARM

PLAN
of
STRETCHERS

SECTION
A-A

CHAIR UPHOLSTERED
IN PETIT POINT

DOTTED LINES SHOW
EXPOSED FRAMEWORK
AT BACK.

FRONT

SIDE

CENTER LINE OF CHAIR

CROMWELLIAN TYPE ARM CHAIR
English about 1660 (Walnut)
NOW IN THE METROPOLITAN MUSEUM OF ART

LEATHER-COVERED CHAIR
American 1625-1675

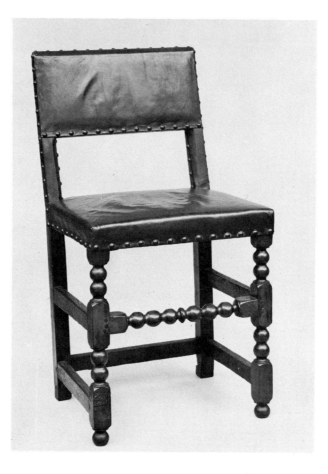

THIS chair of American Colonial execution is similar in type to that shown on the preceding plate. It is of the severe and angular construction favored at this period and reflects a spirit of honest and conscientious craftsmanship.

Its shallow padded seat and squat back panels are upholstered in leather held in place by rows of brass headed nails and covered in a like material are the connecting portions of the back supports.

The framing of knob-turned work, as developed in this chair, is from an earlier English source than is the spiral turnings. Both manners of treating chair frames, however, gained popularity abroad and in our colonies, and occasionally the two methods, knob-turning and spiral-turning, were employed in the same frame.

Although English prototypes of this example were generally constructed of oak, walnut and other local woods were also used in their Colonial adaptations. Witness the maple used in this particular chair.

In addition to the employment of leather as upholstery, Turkeywork and other fine textiles came into general use about the middle of the 17th century.

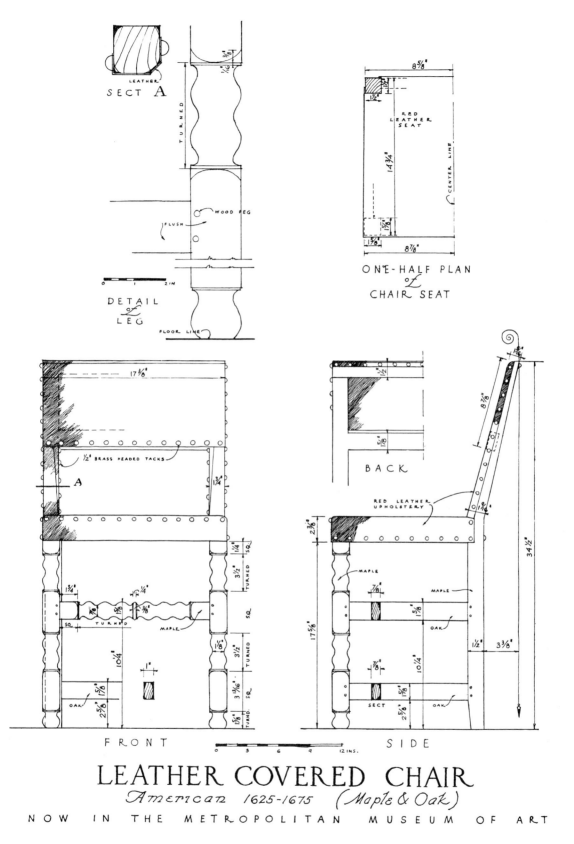

SECT A

LEATHER

DETAIL
of
LEG

TURNED

WOOD PEG

FLUSH

FLOOR LINE

0   1   2 IN

ONE-HALF PLAN
of
CHAIR SEAT

RED
LEATHER
SEAT

CENTER LINE

8⅝"

14¾"

8⅞"

17⅜"

½" BRASS HEADED TACKS

A

BACK

RED LEATHER
UPHOLSTERY

MAPLE

MAPLE

OAK

MAPLE

TURNED

OAK

SECT

OAK

34½"

8⅞"

17⅝"

10¼"

2⅜"

2⅝"

FRONT

0   3   6   9   12 INS.

SIDE

LEATHER COVERED CHAIR
American 1625-1675 (Maple & Oak)
NOW IN THE METROPOLITAN MUSEUM OF ART

FLEMISH XVII CENTURY CHAIR

THIS high backed side chair executed in Flanders in the 17th century is of walnut, a wood then used as the principal alternative of oak. The low seat of ample proportions is upholstered in petit point—the French were at this time keen patrons of the art of tapestry weaving—which is fixed to the frame with large brass-headed tacks. The raked uprights of the back are tapered to the top where they terminate in a simple cut-out design. These back supports are connected by three broad horizontal rails, slightly curved in plan, and of an interesting cut-out pattern of reversed curves. The front legs and underbracing are turned in a full, sturdy pattern of the vase, ring and bulb with a finial of characteristic turning surmounting the middle of the central stretcher.

The contrast between the easy flowing lines of the horizontal splats of the back and the close, full turnings of the legs and braces gives to this chair a quaint charm. But, in spite of its simplicity of line, it is quite elegant in style and is enriched with a tapestry of an over-all floral pattern of rich and mellow tones.

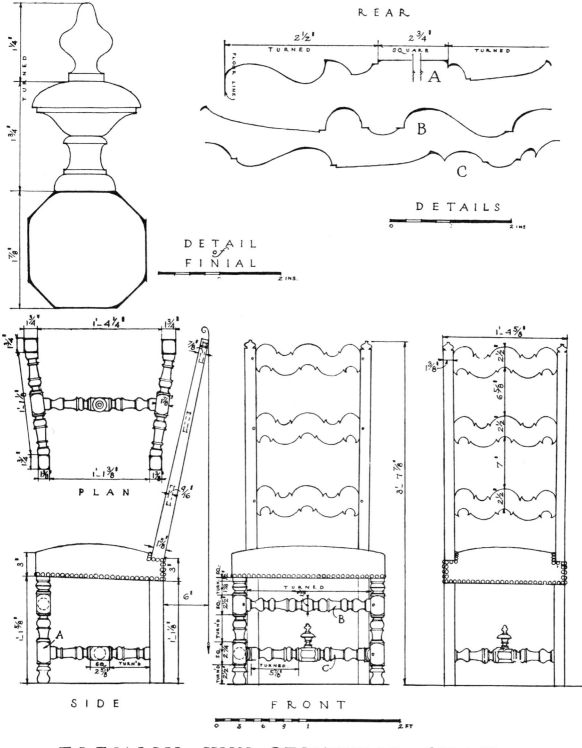

REAR

DETAILS

DETAIL FINIAL

PLAN

SIDE

FRONT

FLEMISH XVII CENTURY CHAIR
Walnut upholstered in Petit Point
NOW IN THE METROPOLITAN MUSEUM OF ART

CHARLES II SIDE CHAIR

English 1670-1680

A NEW style of furniture was introduced in England during the reign of Charles II, the predominating note of which was the influence of fashions imported from the countries of Europe. The changes in proportion, garnishment and contour are faithfully shown in the chairs of this period.

The back of the Flemish Stuart chair illustrated is high and narrow, and, as was the custom after 1660, has panelwork of cane between the broad, carved uprights of the splat. The main supports of the back are of turned wood, this treatment also extending to the front legs which terminate in scroll feet turning outward, a feature borrowed from the Flemish. The broad, horizontal rails uniting the back at the top and bottom of the splat effect and also the front understretcher are ornamented with an elaborate and pretentious design in carved and pierced work. The carved scroll and floral pattern, the latter usually representing a Tudor rose, was imported from Holland and used universally by the English artisans of this time.

Although this period is sometimes called the "Walnut Period," other woods including maple, beech and oak were employed. This particular chair is made of beech.

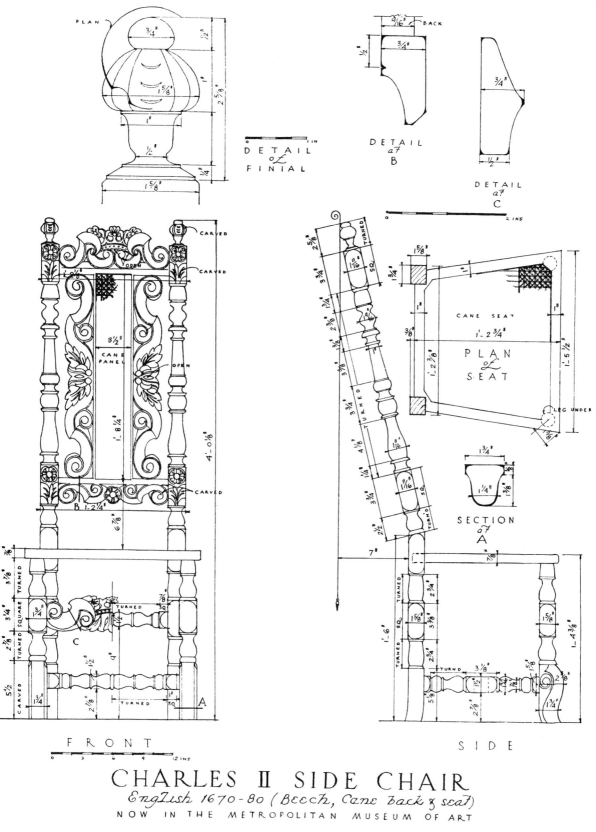

DETAIL
of
FINIAL

DETAIL
at
B

DETAIL
at
C

FRONT

SIDE

CHARLES II SIDE CHAIR
English 1670-80 (Beech, Cane back & seat)
NOW IN THE METROPOLITAN MUSEUM OF ART

CHAISE LONGUE
American Late XVII Century

DETAILS introduced from Flanders under the reign of William and Mary were boldly reflected in both the turning and carving of the furniture of early America.

In this maple Carolean chaise longue or day-bed, an article of furniture then in common use, are incorporated some of the typical Flemish and rococo motifs so much in favor at this time. This is emphatically evidenced by the use of the so-called Flemish scroll, or S-scroll, elaborately if rather crudely, carved in the openwork cresting rail and in the stretchers, and also by the turnings of the legs with their rather sturdy interpretation of the vase or baluster form. These legs are termi-

nated by ball shaped feet, while the main back supports, topped at the cresting rail with turned finials of urn derivation, are indicative of a column of classic proportions.

From this period date many chairs and couches in which cane was used for the seats and backs, a practice that was introduced in Europe from India. They were first called Cane or India chairs.

Day-beds such as this example, which were intended to be placed against a wall, have only one stretcher decorated, while those designed to be seen from all sides were fitted with two ornamental stretchers.

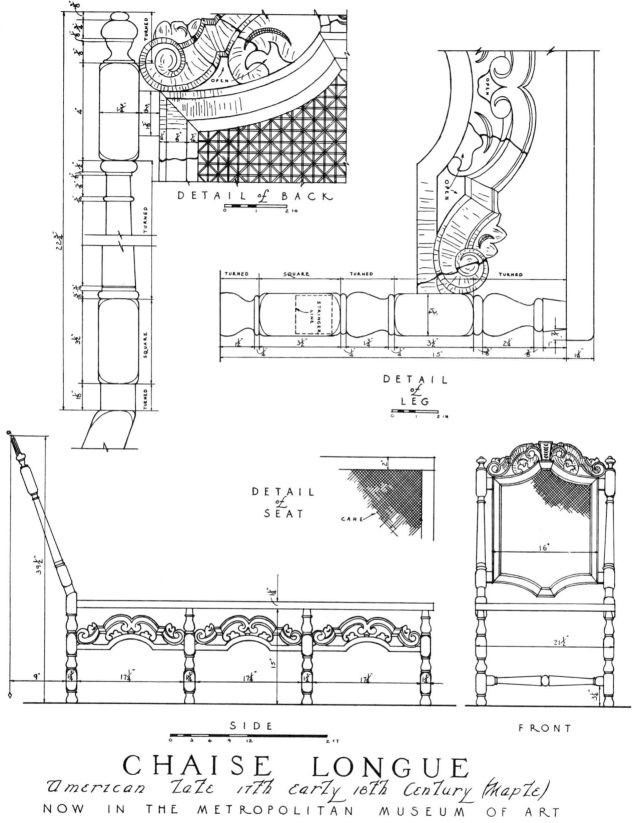

DETAIL of BACK

0 1 2 IN

DETAIL of LEG

0 1 2 IN

DETAIL of SEAT

CANE

SIDE

0 3 6 9 12   2 FT

FRONT

CHAISE LONGUE
American Late 17th early 18th Century (Maple)
NOW IN THE METROPOLITAN MUSEUM OF ART

BANISTER BACK CHAIR
American 1700-1725

DURING the reign of Queen Anne, in the early 18th century, the banister back chair was developed from earlier and more simple types. The characteristics of this chair are found in the straight and high backs which was frequently adorned with a carved head piece of scroll design. The legs and uprights were turned and the seats were of woven rush. The most interesting feature of this type of chair and the one from which it derives its name is the banister back, made of four upright spindles, each one-half a banister, with the smooth, flat side toward the front and the back rounded.

The spacious chair shown here is of unusually fine proportions, with flat, broad seat and slender, graceful arms resting upon turned uprights of good design. The broad, fluted foot with a slight turn outward is of Spanish origin, a feature borrowed from the Spanish Stuart chair, which preceded this style. The bulbous turning of the underbracing is another feature to be found in this type.

The wood used is maple, which has been stained to a walnut color.

The workmanship on these chairs was not brought to the fine finish of the later pieces but suggests a true and simpler craftsmanship.

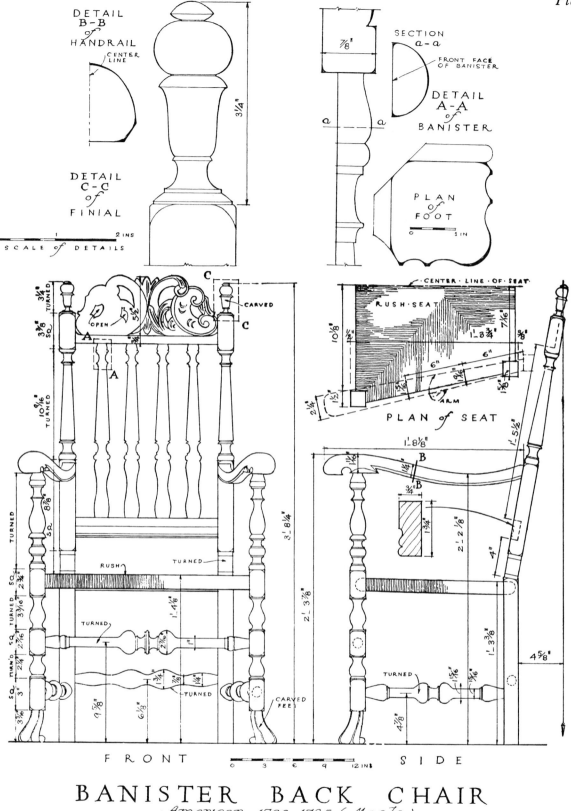

DETAIL
B - B
of
HANDRAIL

CENTER
LINE

DETAIL
C - C
of
FINIAL

3¼"

0   1   2 INS
SCALE of DETAILS

7/8"

SECTION
a - a

FRONT FACE
OF BANISTER

DETAIL
A - A
of
BANISTER

a   a

PLAN
of
FOOT

0   1 IN

FRONT

SIDE

0   3   6   9   12 INS

BANISTER BACK CHAIR
American 1700-1725 (Maple)
NOW IN THE METROPOLITAN MUSEUM OF ART

LOUIS XIV ARM CHAIR
French 1643-1715

UNDER the patronage of Louis XIV the arts of France were carried to magnificent luxury. It is to the credit of this monarch that the decorative arts were put on a plane with painting, architecture and sculpture, from which resulted the fine art of furniture making in France and the perfection of its workmanship.

The decorative treatment of the furniture of this period was based upon the combination of the straight line and the curve. The general proportions gave a feeling of strength and breadth. In the chair shown on these pages the supports and arms of walnut are in the form of large, sweeping scrolls with the outer surfaces carved in low relief with shells, ample scrolls, and acanthus leaves in restrained and graceful patterns. The underframing, an adaptation of the X form, is composed of reversed curves, enriched with carving.

The impetus given to the art of cabinet making under Louis XIV was also extended to that of tapestry weaving. Upholstery was greatly in favor and was therefore almost invariably used on the fauteuils or arm chairs of this period. Frequently gold and silver headed nails held the tapestry in place.

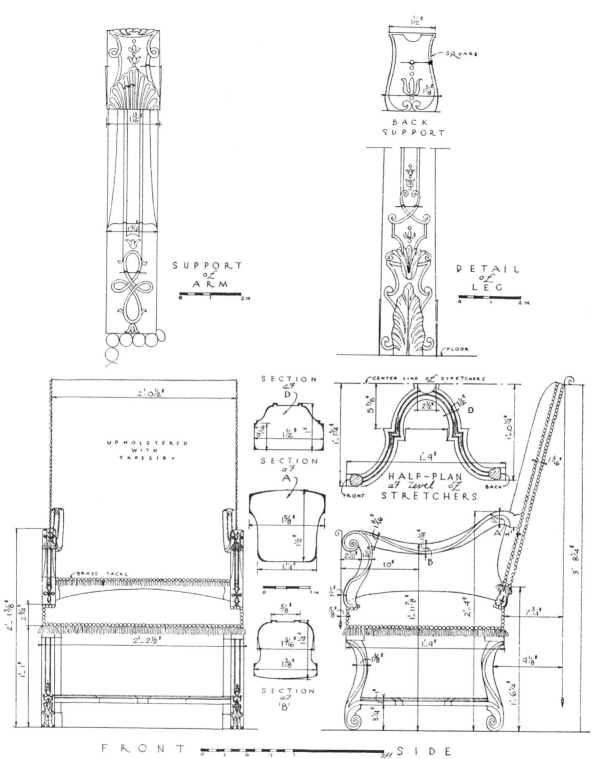

SUPPORT
of
ARM

BACK
SUPPORT

DETAIL
of
LEG

FRONT — SIDE

LOUIS XIV ARM CHAIR
French 1643-1715 (Carved Walnut)
NOW IN THE METROPOLITAN MUSEUM OF ART

WINDSOR ARM CHAIR

English 1775-1800

THE Windsor or "turned" chair, whose popularity has remained unabated to the present time, was developed during the reign of Queen Anne. Graceful simplicity of line and elimination of detail together with sincere and staunch construction are no doubt responsible for the favoritism shown this type of chair. Particularly is this true of its adoption in the colonies, where ease of production, combined with its durable and pleasant character, caused it to develop to a greater degree than in England.

There were many types of Windsor chairs, among them being the fan and comb-back and the bow or hooped-back, to which latter group this specimen belongs. Practically every member of a Windsor chair is turned, and in this case, the spindles at the back and also the legs and stretchers are of bamboo turnings. The seat is hollowed out into a saddle form, a feature almost invariably used in the fashioning of these "turned" types.

Local woods such as ash, oak, hickory and pine were combined in different parts. Hickory, because of its strength, was often used to form the small turned spindles of the back.

Originally this style of chair was made for use out of doors, and was in consequence painted to withstand the weather. Although grey and green were the most favored colors, this example appears in a coat of red.

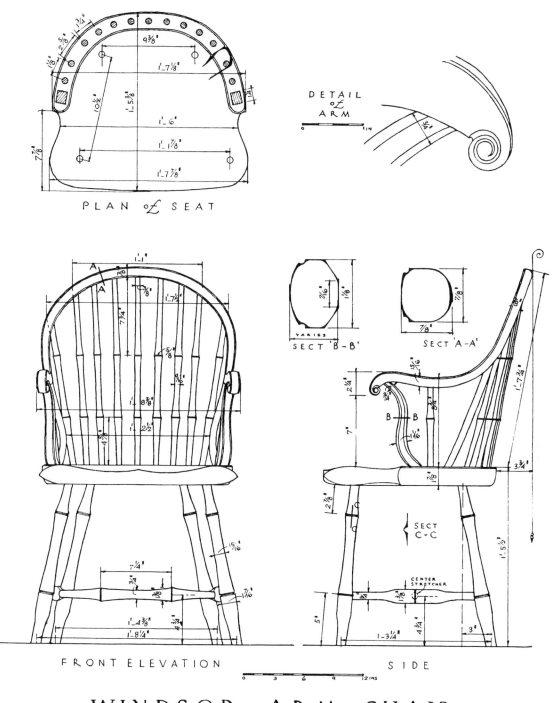

PLAN of SEAT

DETAIL of ARM

SECT 'B-B'

SECT 'A-A'

SECT C-C

CENTER STRETCHER

FRONT ELEVATION

SIDE

WINDSOR ARM CHAIR
English 1775 to 1800 (Maple & Hickory)
NOW IN THE METROPOLITAN MUSEUM OF ART

SPLAT-BACK SIDE CHAIR

American 1725-1750

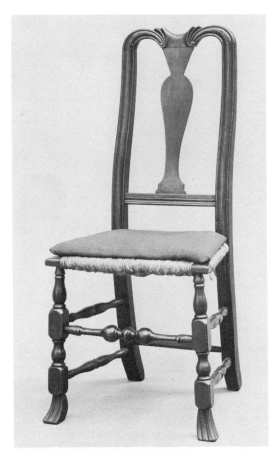

THE 18th century ushered into the American Colonies this type of side chair. It is a combination of Queen Anne and Dutch styles with a solid, vase-shaped splat back, frequently called "fiddle-back," and with curved cresting rail and rush seat. The back supports are moulded from a few inches below the seat and terminate in graceful curves to embrace the cresting motif. Spanish feet support the two front legs, which, in their turnings of baluster form, demonstrate the manner of decorating rectangular joinery most characteristic of this period.

The selection of maple follows prevailing custom, except that in the present instance chestnut is used for fashioning the front legs and stretchers. As added variety spruce is employed in the upper side stretchers.

The Dutch style played an important role in the work of the early Colonists, due in all probability to the many splendid artisans among the Dutch settlers. This influence, together with that of William and Mary and Queen Anne, was pronounced until the middle of the 18th century when it was gradually supplanted by that of the early Georgian and Chippendale.

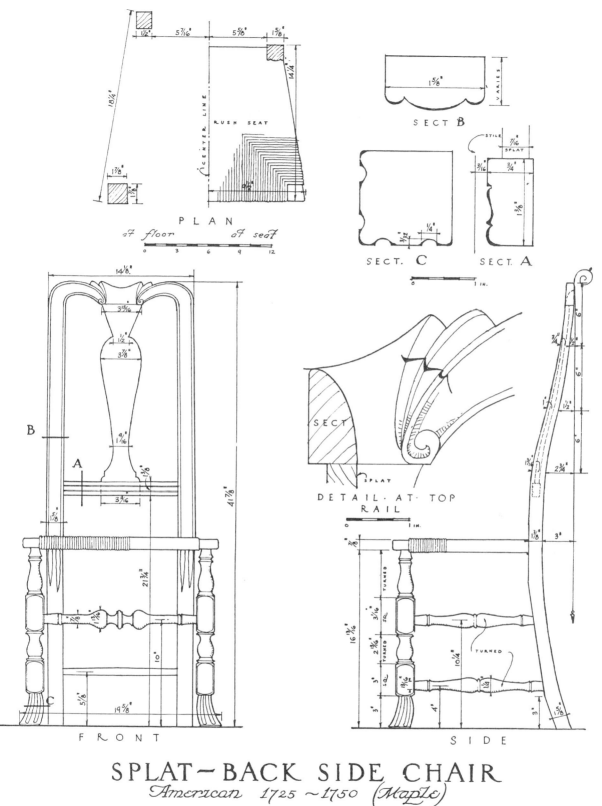

PLAN

of floor   of seat

0   3   6   9   12

SECT B

SECT. C   SECT. A

DETAIL · AT · TOP
RAIL

FRONT

SIDE

SPLAT~BACK SIDE CHAIR
American 1725 ~ 1750 (Maple)
NOW · IN · THE · METROPOLITAN MUSEUM OF · ART

ARM CHAIR, STYLE OF QUEEN ANNE
English 1702-1714

THE principal characteristics of the style of furniture known as "Queen Anne" are the cabriole leg, sturdy, ample proportions and undulating lines, with surfaces for the most part plain and devoid of garnishment and the grain of the wood relied upon to give enrichment. Walnut was the wood most generally employed. When ornament was used it was generally confined to various interpretations of the shell.

The idea of comfort is predominant in this furniture, expressing itself particularly in rounded corners and broad ample seats covered with upholstery.

The arm chair illustrated on these two pages is of English origin and an excellent example of the early Queen Anne style with its high hooped back whose side frames form incomplete S-scrolls, and with the cabriole leg which, in the early 18th century in England, reached the most perfect stage of its development. A boldly carved shell in large scallops decorates the knee of the cabriole leg which terminates in the plain club or pad foot, especially characteristic of the earlier portion of this particular reign. The broad central splat is of the fiddle pattern and the arms are comfortably shaped in a horizontal curve and supported by an upright ornamented with an acanthus leaf carved in low relief.

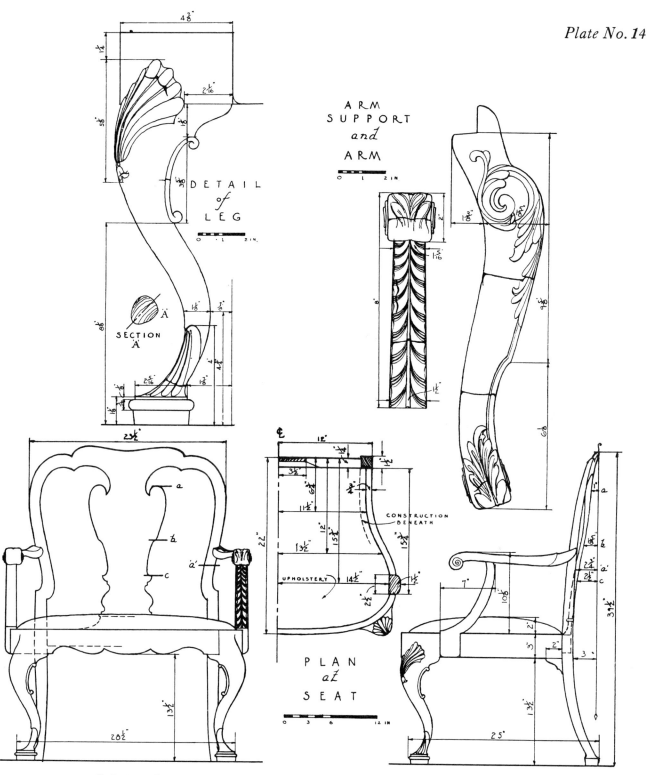

DETAIL of LEG

ARM SUPPORT and ARM

SECTION "A"

CONSTRUCTION BENEATH

UPHOLSTERY

PLAN at SEAT

FRONT

SIDE

ARM CHAIR *Style of* QUEEN ANNE
English 1702 – 1714 (Walnut)
NOW IN THE METROPOLITAN MUSEUM OF ART

QUEEN ANNE SETTEE

English 1710-1720

DURING the Queen Anne period settees were held in much esteem and a high order of craftsmanship was displayed in their execution by the cabinet makers of that time. Their settees were remarkable for their comfort and yet extremely graceful. This grace was obtained with a very sparing use of ornamentation.

The framework of the model selected rests upon six legs. These are of the cabriole type. This typical leg treatment, brought from the East by the Dutch, was perfected under the reign of Queen Anne and remained in favor for about one hundred years. Stretchers connecting the legs were generally discarded in the early years of the 18th century. At this time, also, wooden arms were again used and in conjunction with upholstered backs as well as those of wood.

In this English example the seat frame is straight with rounded corners and with an inset upholstered seat. The outward flaring, shaped arms, resting upon a C-scroll support attached to the sides of the seat frame, are indicative of this style, as is also the claw-and-ball foot which came into prominence during the later years of this period.

The contour of the high, upholstered back which is slightly tilted is formed by two cyma curves which rise to embrace a central curve of elliptical form. The cyma curve was consistently used in the design of furniture during this reign. At this time, also, chair backs and seats were covered in exquisite needlework, in damasks, velvets and brocades. Chintz was used in the less pretentious articles.

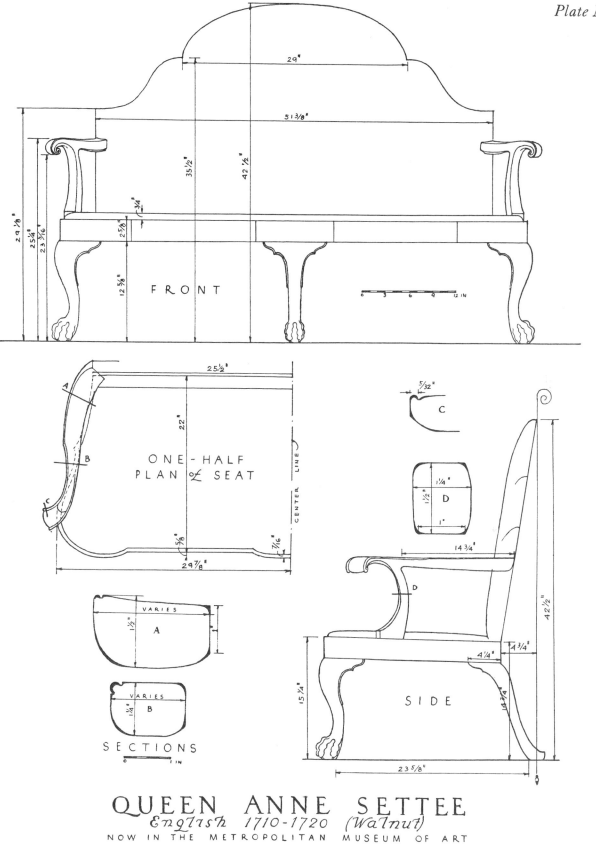

FRONT

ONE-HALF
PLAN of SEAT

SECTIONS

SIDE

QUEEN ANNE SETTEE
English 1710-1720 (Walnut)
NOW IN THE METROPOLITAN MUSEUM OF ART

AMERICAN EASY CHAIR

1725-1750

THIS chair of portly dimensions is of the type known as "Grandfather's Chair," "Easy Chair" and "Saddlecheck Chair." Chairs of this description were made during the 18th century in various styles, with Dutch, Chippendale and Hepplewhite legs. They were heavily upholstered with deep, broad, cushioned seat and low arms. The backs were high with ears or wings extending forward at the sides as a protection against draughts, since these chairs were generally used near the fireside.

The illustration shows an easy chair with short cabriole legs and the claw and ball foot of the Queen Anne style, with heads of the American eagle carved in low relief upon the knees. Both the legs and the strong braces are of mahogany. The fronts of the arms are finished in both a horizontal and vertical scroll, a feature of the early form of this kind of chair.

The upholstering is of leather fastened at all edges with brass-headed nails very closely spaced. It was not uncommon, however, for these chairs to be covered with chintz, with a deep flounce or ruffle nearly hiding the feet.

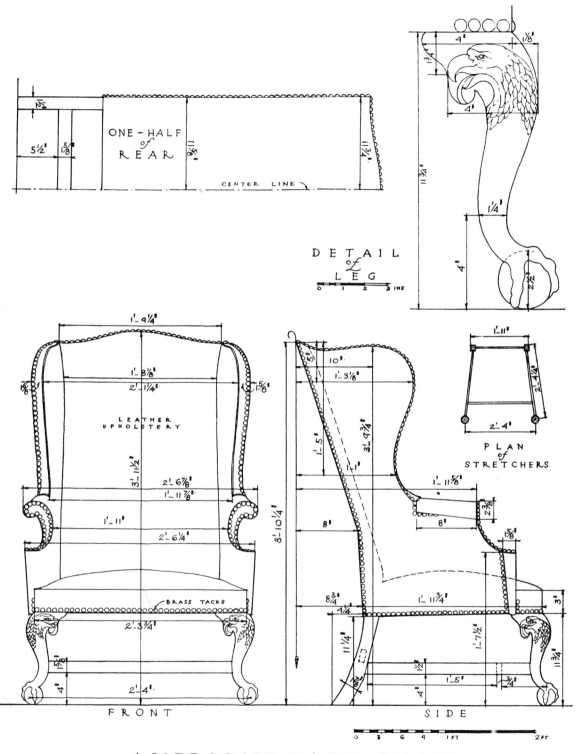

ONE–HALF
of
REAR

CENTER LINE

DETAIL
of
LEG

0   1   2   3 INS

LEATHER
UPHOLSTERY

BRASS TACKS

PLAN
of
STRETCHERS

FRONT

SIDE

0   3   6   9   1 FT   2 FT

AMERICAN EASY CHAIR
Mahogany about 1725-50
NOW IN THE METROPOLITAN MUSEUM OF ART

PORTUGUESE CHAIR

AN elegant version of a Portuguese adaptation of the Queen Anne vogue is this side chair with its fiddle-splatted back of high hooped design and its use of the cabriole leg. Following the custom of the time and true to its prototypes, the ample seat is flaring with rounded corners at the front and is provided with a rebated seat covered in upholstery and fitted into a rail of shaped outline. The four cabriole legs end in a form of foot most typical of the earlier years of the Queen Anne period, that of the "Dutch" or club type. The back is spooned in profile with the uprights breaking a short distance above the seat frame and forming concave curves which terminate in the hooped top.

The common motif of carved decoration of this period, the cockle-shell, has been unsparingly used on this chair on the juncture of the legs and seat rail, and also at the upper portion of the central splat. The framework members of the back are richly moulded in a manner somewhat contrary to usual conception. The pronounced use of the C-scroll is also an inherent characteristic of these times.

In contradiction to the customary use of walnut for the execution of furniture of this origin, this side chair is fashioned of ironwood.

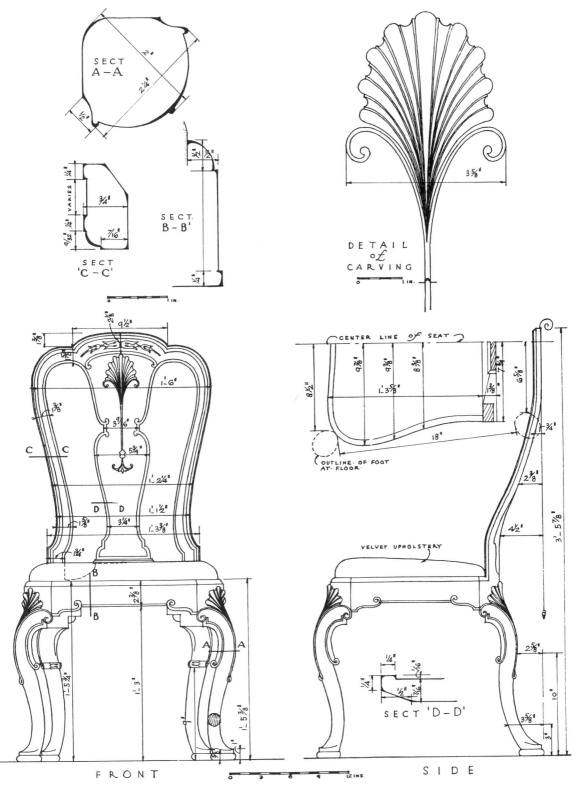

SECT A–A

SECT. B–B'

SECT 'C–C'

DETAIL
of
CARVING

3 5/8"

FRONT

SIDE

CENTER LINE OF SEAT

OUTLINE OF FOOT AT FLOOR

VELVET UPHOLSTERY

SECT 'D–D'

PORTUGESE CHAIR
Early XVIII. century (Ironwood).

LOUIS XV ARM CHAIR

French 1723-1774

THE general trend of furniture design during the reign of Louis XV (1715-1774) was toward comfort, luxury and abandon. This, of all periods, was the most characteristically French. To charm the society of that time it was necessary that the furniture designs should reflect the graciousness, seductiveness and exuberance of the court life of that pleasure loving monarch.

The supremacy of the curvilinear over the straight lines of the preceding style is pronounced; in fact, wherever possible, the construction is curved with serpentine or swelling fronts and with graceful lines swinging into opposing curves. Balance was generally obtained, not through symmetry, but by the disposition of curves and ornamentation.

Shells, flowers, scrolls, foliage and flame motifs were among the most characteristic forms of decoration. These were used at random with the most audacious freedom. The decoration of this period was typically rococo.

Comfort and ease governed the proportions of the chairs, this particular piece of furniture being the index of the Louis XV style. The seats and backs were broad and broken into curves. The legs were generally of the cabriole type enriched with carving and terminating at the foot in a small scroll, leaf or dolphin's head. Luxurious and intricate carving ornamented the seat rails, back frame and arms of these chairs. Caning as well as upholstery was used on the backs and seats, such as is seen in the example illustrated.

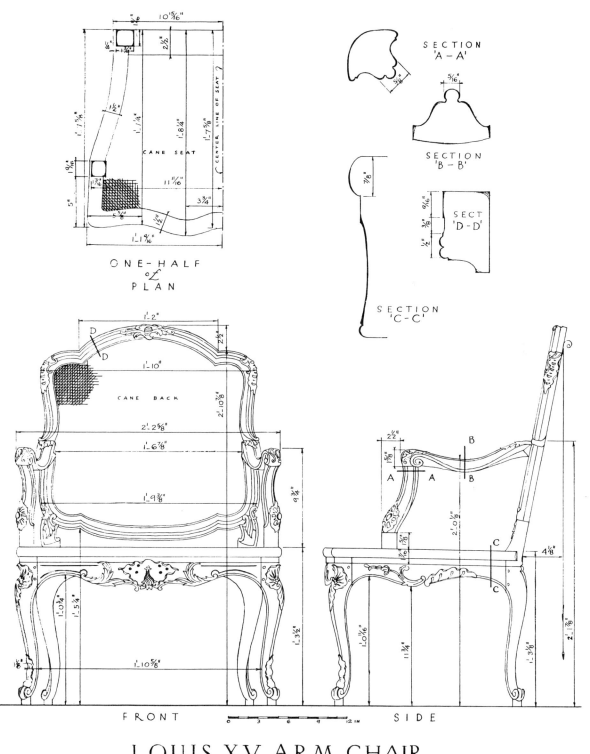

SECTION 'A - A'

SECTION 'B - B'

SECTION 'C - C'

SECT 'D - D'

CANE SEAT

CENTER LINE OF SEAT

ONE-HALF
of
PLAN

CANE BACK

FRONT

SIDE

LOUIS XV ARM CHAIR
French 1723-74 (Beechwood and Cane)
NOW IN THE METROPOLITAN MUSEUM OF ART

LOUIS XV CHAISE LONGUE
French Last Half XVIII Century

THE chaise longue of the period of Louis Quinze followed the same general lines of contour and ornament as were incorporated in the chairs of this style. The frame-work of this particular couch or day-bed exemplifies the flexibility and sophistication of this school of design. The seat framing shows restraint in its handsome carving and is broken into many sinuous curves which graciously flow into cabriole legs terminating in tapered feet.

Upholstery is applied to the scrolled and rolled-over arms and to the seat frame. Over the latter is provided a removable stuffed cushion and small cylindrical cushions are placed at either end to ease the comfortless outward swing of the arm scrolls. In lieu of an upholstered back three separate cushions of ample and uniform size are intended for use against the wall.

The delicately carved woodwork, which was often painted and gilded, adds gentleness and charm and forms a delightful framework for the rich colors of the upholstery. The accompanying example was originally painted.

Woods employed at this time comprised mainly walnut, oak, mahogany and cherry with various other woods for inlaying. However, this piece of furniture and that shown on the preceding plate were fashioned of beechwood.

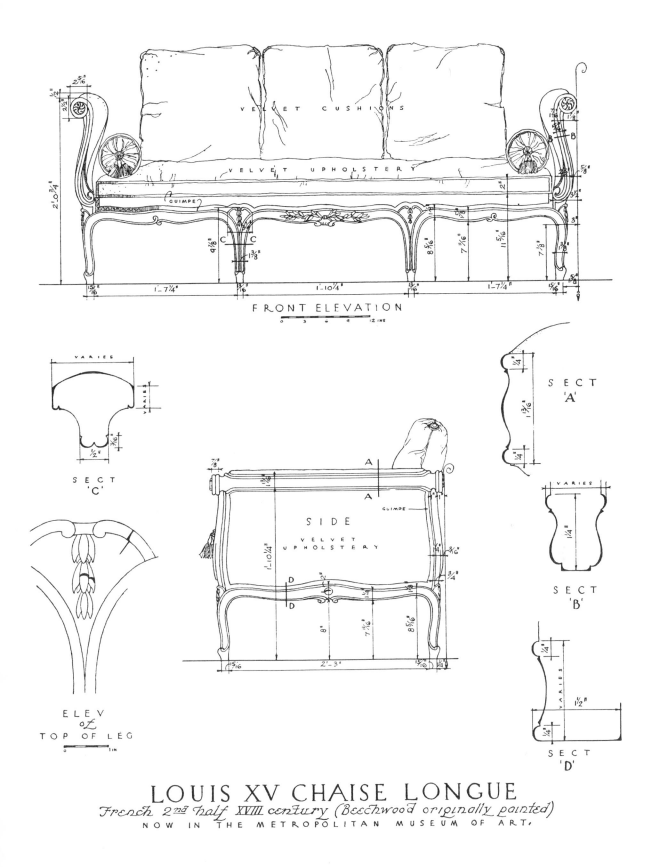

FRONT ELEVATION

VELVET CUSHIONS

VELVET UPHOLSTERY

GUIMPE

SECT 'A'

SECT 'B'

SECT 'C'

SECT 'D'

SIDE
VELVET UPHOLSTERY

GUIMPE

ELEV of TOP OF LEG

VARIES

LOUIS XV CHAISE LONGUE
French 2nd half XVIII century (Beechwood originally painted)
NOW IN THE METROPOLITAN MUSEUM OF ART.

DOUBLE CHAIR, STYLE OF CHIPPENDALE

English

IN the workshop of the three Chippendales— father, son and grandson—were made some of the most excellent examples of English cabinet work. Skilful craftsmanship was here combined with an artistry which subsequently changed the spirit of furniture design. The first of the Chippendales was not only a skilful artist-craftsman but a brilliant carver, who developed characteristics that persist throughout the style bearing his name. However, the name Chippendale usually implies the second of the three cabinet makers.

Furniture of this style may be roughly classed under the various influences which were brought to bear upon it, that is, Queen Anne; French of Louis Quatorze and the Regency; Classic; the Chinese with variations of classic, Louis Quinze or Gothic motifs; and Gothic. Several influences were at times manifested in one piece of furniture, but although this style underwent many transformations the furniture of the Chippendale school can invariably be recognized, so marked are its characteristics.

This mahogany settee of double chair form was executed in England about the middle of the 18th century and in it the French influence is the controlling impulse. It is of the splat back type with a Cupid's bow top rail. The splat of interlaced strapping is relieved by carving in the French manner of acanthus leaves. The legs are of the cabriole type and terminate in carved scrolls.

The single chair back-motif is practically preserved complete, with each upright of the back carried down separately to the seat, leaving the top rail as the only connecting link.

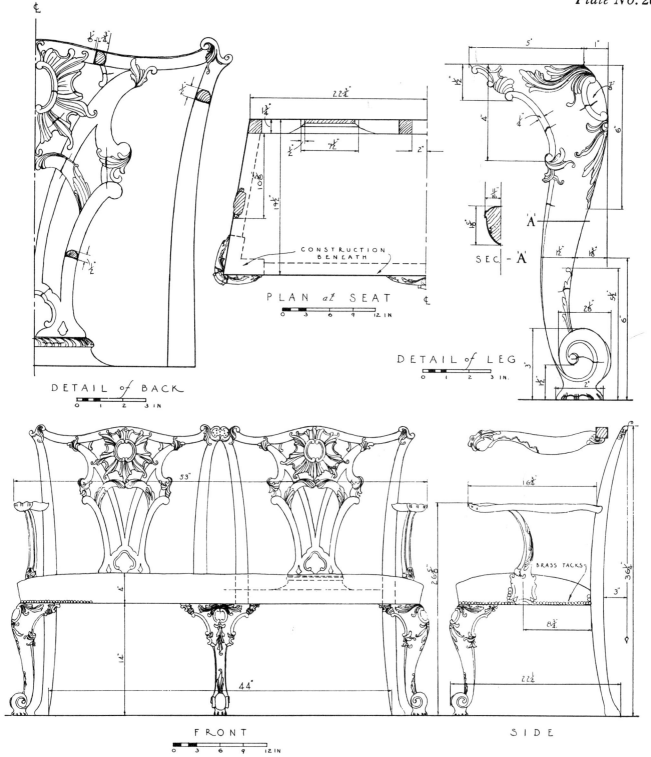

PLAN at SEAT

CONSTRUCTION BENEATH

DETAIL of BACK

0   1   2   3 IN

SEC - 'A'

DETAIL of LEG

0   1   2   3 IN.

BRASS TACKS

FRONT

0   3   6   9   12 IN

SIDE

DOUBLE CHAIR *Style of* CHIPPENDALE
English (Mahogany)
NOW IN THE MUSEUM OF RHODE ISLAND SCHOOL OF DESIGN

STOOL, STYLE OF CHIPPENDALE

English 1725-1775

OF the same inspiration as that of the preceding plate is this commodious stool, which at this period was an article of furniture of rather infrequent occurrence.

The seat is shaped in a serpentine effect on the major sides and is of the "stitched-up" type, that is, the upholstery conceals the entire seat frame and is held in place at the lower edges of the rail by a row of brass headed nails.

Legs of these Chippendale style stools followed the same evolution as those of contemporaneous chairs and are in this instance of the cabriole or bandy-leg type, ending in a modified scroll foot.

It is interesting to note that in this model the leg proper is moulded and not, therefore, exactly cylindrical in section.

The rococo carving at the knee is of particular interest in that it is a composite of two differing motifs, a carved flame on one side and a wave somewhat resembling the hair of the lion's mane, on the other. The favored C-scroll is here freely used and forms, by a clever combination of opposed curves, the inner outline of the legs and brackets.

Following the general rule of Chippendale furniture, this stool is made of mahogany.

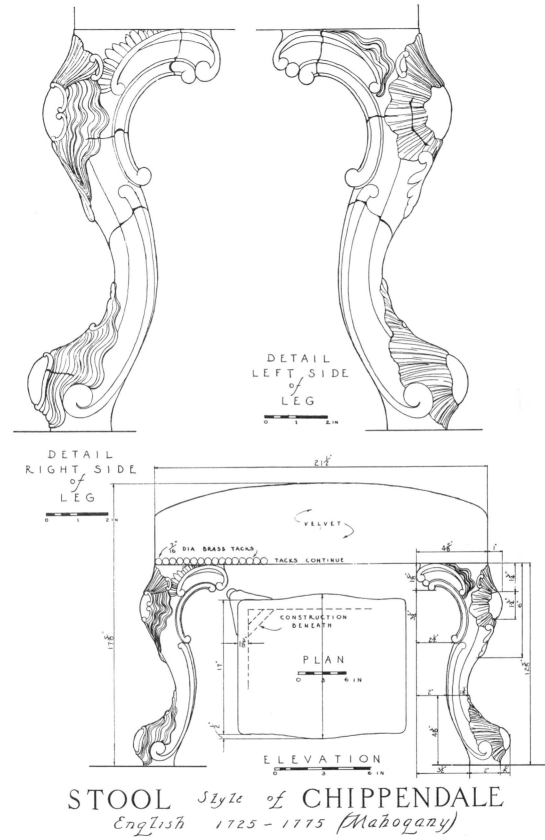

DETAIL
LEFT SIDE
of
LEG

0   1   2 IN

DETAIL
RIGHT SIDE
of
LEG

0   1   2 IN

21½"

VELVET

2/16 DIA BRASS TACKS

TACKS CONTINUE

4⅜"   1"

CONSTRUCTION
BENEATH

PLAN

0   3   6 IN

17"

17⅝

ELEVATION

0   3   6 IN

STOOL *Style* of CHIPPENDALE
English   1725 - 1775 (Mahogany)

NOW IN THE MUSEUM OF RHODE ISLAND SCHOOL OF DESIGN

CHIPPENDALE STYLE CHAIR
American About 1760-1770

THE ladder-back design, which developed from the slat type, was one of the various methods employed by the versatile Chippendale for decorating chair backs. This style consists of three or four horizontal rungs, similarly spaced, and connecting the back framework. The accompanying example is one typical of this mode of construction and ornamentation with its four pierced and moulded rungs shaped to form gracefully interlacing serpentine curves.

Square legs, which were the most usual type employed by Chippendale, succeeded those of cabriole form terminating in the claw-and-ball foot. Stretcher work was added to these square legged models to brace the under structure. Frequently combined with this style of leg framing was the back of ladder design, which resulted in the style of side chair under discussion.

The severity of line produced by the rectangular seat and leg framing was somewhat mitigated by the introduction of small ovolo beaded mouldings, such as the softening of the angle at the outer vertical edge of the front legs by the use of this vertical moulding.

It has been said of Chippendale that, through his inspired mastery of the art of wood carving, he made history "in the realm of constructive outline."

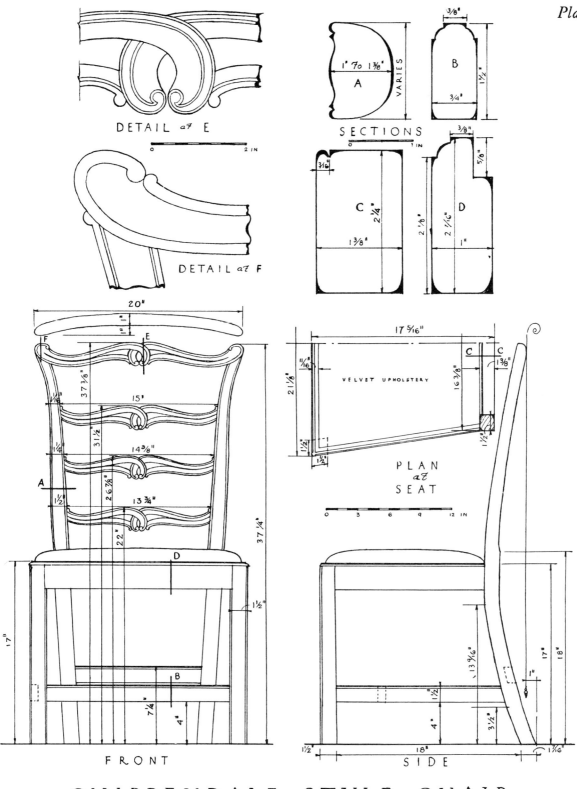

DETAIL at E

DETAIL at F

SECTIONS

A — 1' To 1⅜" — VARIES

B — ⅜" — ¾" — 1½"

C — 3/16" — 2¼" — 1⅜"

D — ⅜" — 5/8" — 2⅛" — 2¼" — 1"

FRONT

20"
1"
1"
37⅛"
15"
31½"
14⅜"
26⅞"
13¾"
22"
37¼"
⅛"
¼"
1½"
1½"
7¼"
4"
17"

PLAN at SEAT

17 5/16"
VELVET UPHOLSTERY
21⅛"
16⅜"
1⅜"
11/16"
½"
½"
½"

0 3 6 9 12 IN

SIDE

½"
18"
1 1/16"
13 9/16"
17"
18"
1"
1½"
4"
3½"

CHIPPENDALE STYLE CHAIR
American about 1760-70 (Mahogany)
NOW IN THE BOSTON MUSEUM OF FINE ARTS

CHIPPENDALE CHAIR

American 1760-1770

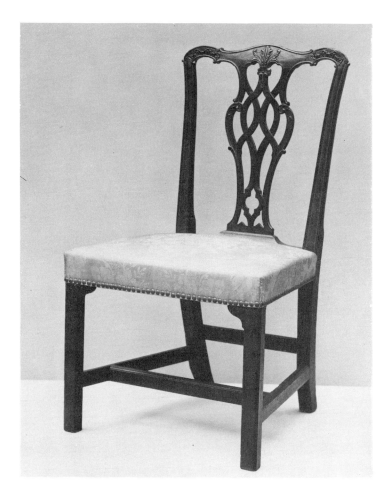

THE style inaugurated by Thomas Chippendale in the middle of the 18th century in England and which persisted for over thirty years is reflected in some of the best Georgian furniture. His chairs retained during this period similar characteristics, namely, the flat, broad, upholstered seat, the chairback slightly narrower at the bottom than at the top, and the intricately pierced and carved splat back. The first type of Chippendale chairs retained the Dutch cabriole leg which was borrowed and perfected from the preceding style. This was followed by a type incorporating certain Louis XV features, mainly in the form and carving of the splat. Then came the ladder back chair, and finally a style employing Chinese and Gothic features in which the lower part of the chair took on lines more nearly square, while the influence of the Dutch and French, as well as those of Gothic and Chinese, became mixed in the design of the back.

It was under this latter influence that the accompanying chair was made. The square, straight legs with their shaped brackets denote the Chinese influence, the form and carvings of the back are Gothic and French, whereas the idea of the splat itself is Dutch.

This chair is executed in a fine-grain, rich-toned mahogany, which came into vogue about this time.

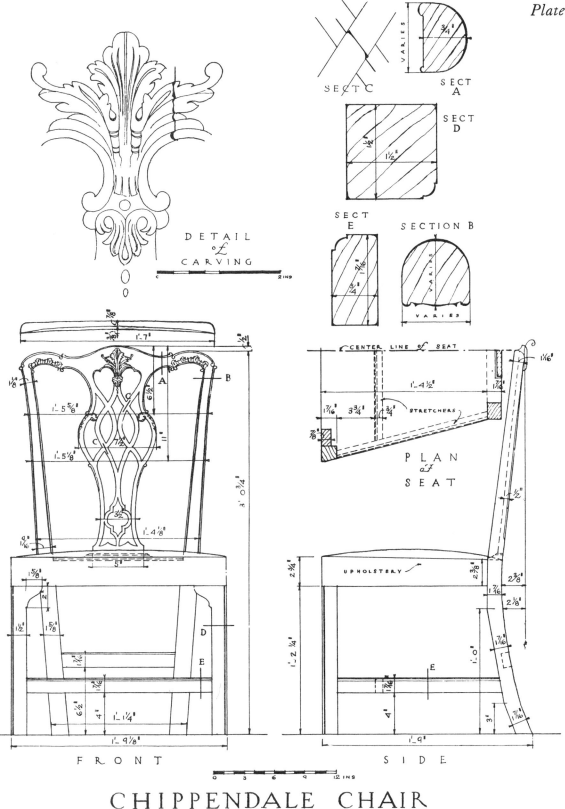

DETAIL of £ CARVING

SECT C

SECT A

SECT D

SECT E

SECTION B

VARIES

CENTER LINE of SEAT

STRETCHERS

PLAN of SEAT

UPHOLSTERY

FRONT

SIDE

0 3 6 9 12 INS

CHIPPENDALE CHAIR
American about 1760-70 (Mahogany)
NOW IN THE METROPOLITAN MUSEUM OF ART

CHIPPENDALE STYLE CHAIR
American Third Quarter XVIII Century

OF especial significance on the chair under consideration is the square framework of seat and leg, enhanced by hybridized fretwork adapted from both Chinese and Gothic sources. On the very broad, straight seat frame a pattern of Chinese fretwork is delicately carved in low relief, whereas on the legs the pointed arch, closely associated with the Gothic style, is introduced and handled and carved in the same manner. The straight legs are slightly chamfered on the inner edge, a method practiced by Chippendale of giving greater delicacy of appearance to these structural members.

In the design and carving of the top rail and carved enrichment, applied to the rather delicate tracery of the intermediate pierced splat, we find an introduction of motifs from France under the reign of Louis Quinze. This chair, certainly, presents a fusion of styles, that of Chinese and Gothic on the framework of the seat and legs, whereas, in the design and ornamentation of the back frame, there is no trace of Oriental influence, but rather, that of late Georgian combined with motifs from France.

The rich design of the splat with its excellent carved decoration forms a balance for the overall ornamentation of the seat rail and leg surfaces.

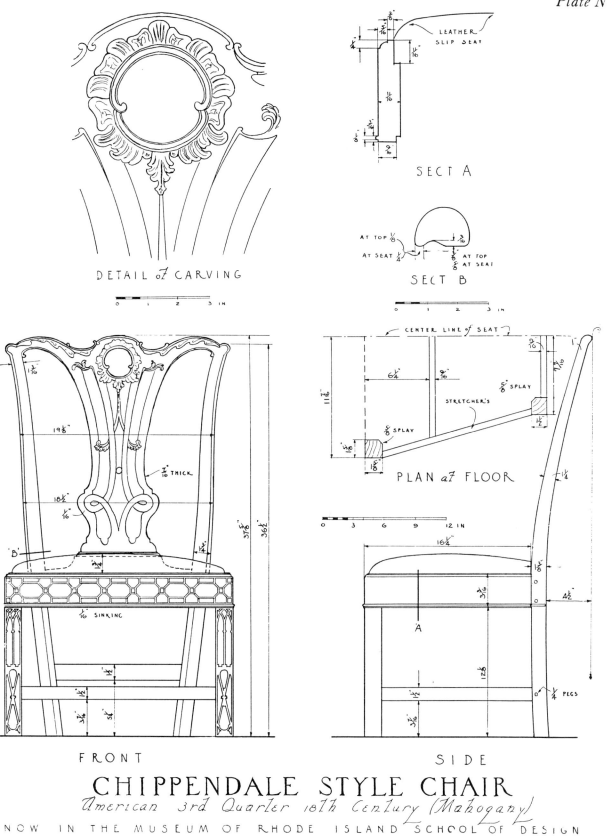

DETAIL of CARVING

SECT A

LEATHER SLIP SEAT

SECT B

PLAN of FLOOR

FRONT

SIDE

CHIPPENDALE STYLE CHAIR
American 3rd Quarter 18th Century (Mahogany)

NOW IN THE MUSEUM OF RHODE ISLAND SCHOOL OF DESIGN

CHIPPENDALE STYLE SOFA
American 1775-1880

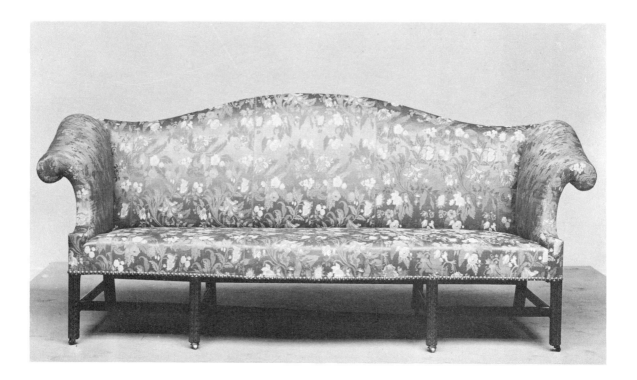

ALTHOUGH the sofa was an article of furniture in common use during the Chippendale era, it was only occasionally made by the Chippendales, due, perhaps, to the limited scope which the upholstery presented for design in comparison with the intricate and ornate patterns of the wooden chair backs of this period. A greater favorite of the Chippendales was the two or three chair-back settees, developed from, and practically a repetition of, the single chair design.

Like the furniture of this time, this example is built upon strong and dignified lines, structurally honest and of good proportions. The frame rested, as a rule, and as in this model, upon eight legs, which are in this example of the straight moulded type and strengthened by straight stretcher work. Carving, of a conventionalized leaf pattern, embellishes the exposed faces of the front four legs.

The outline of the upholstered back is arched in the form of an undulating curve which flows at the ends into bergere wings, or high rolled over arms. The characteristic C-scroll, so much in favor during the regime of Chippendale, is introduced to form the front curve of these flaring wings. High arms, forming a continuation of the back, were adapted from the contemporaneous French taste displayed in Louis XV canapes.

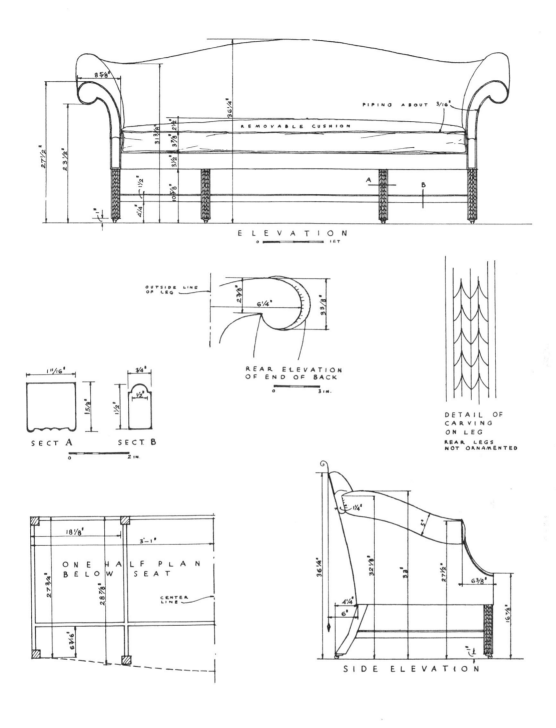

ELEVATION

PIPING ABOUT 3/16"
REMOVABLE CUSHION

REAR ELEVATION
OF END OF BACK

OUTSIDE LINE
OF LEG

SECT. A   SECT. B

DETAIL OF
CARVING
ON LEG
REAR LEGS
NOT ORNAMENTED

ONE HALF PLAN
BELOW SEAT
CENTER LINE

SIDE ELEVATION

CHIPPENDALE STYLE SOFA
American 1775-1800 (Mahogany)
NOW IN THE METROPOLITAN MUSEUM OF ART

CHINTZ-COVERED CHAIR
American

THIS example of "Saddle-check" or "Saddle-cheek" wing chair, although the exact date of its manufacture is uncertain, is undoubtedly of Chippendale influence. It is a further development of the Grandfather chair of earlier date which embodies characteristic lines and motifs of the Queen Anne period, such as the carved eagle at the knee of the cabriole leg.

In the present example, the wings and shaped tops are more flamboyant in their graceful curves; the C-scroll of the upholstered arms of the earlier example has been modified; and the legs have become straight and tapering and are tipped with casters of brass. The slip seat, fitted around the flaring arms, continued in favor from the Queen Anne period, although many examples of this earlier date as well as of the time of the Chippendales indicate that the seat was frequently uncushioned.

Materials in various variety were used at this period for upholstering. Damasks, woolen and linen fabrics of diverse weave, needle-work, brocatelles were equally in favor. Towards the middle of the 18th century in the American colonies calicoes, printed cottons, and chintzes were in use as chair coverings.

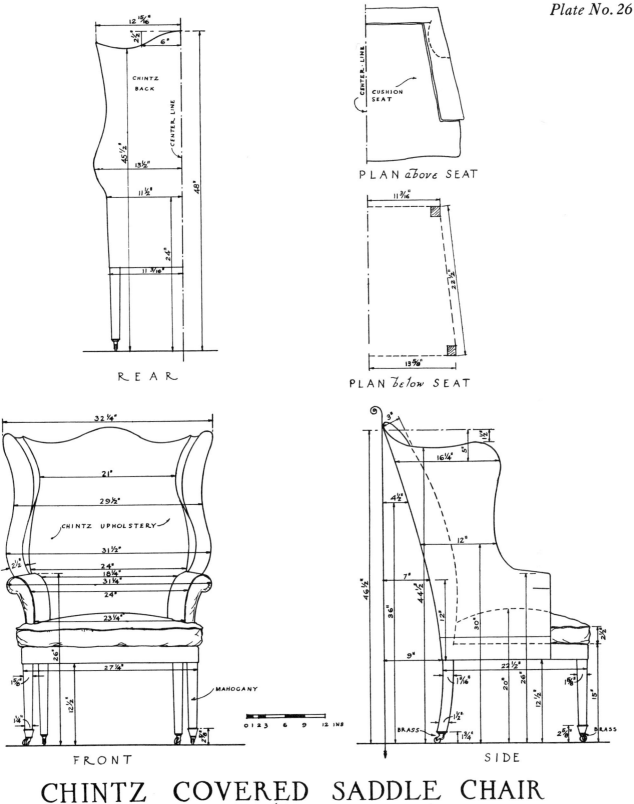

REAR

PLAN *above* SEAT

PLAN *below* SEAT

FRONT

SIDE

CHINTZ COVERED SADDLE CHAIR
American (Mahogany Frame)

NOW IN THE ESSEX INSTITUTE, SALEM MASS

HEPPLEWHITE STYLE CHAIR
American 1785-1795

THIS American-made chair, with its pleasing lines and well placed decoration, combines many of the chief features of the Hepplewhite style of rather late date. The shield-back, a device originally taken from the Crusader's shield and adopted by Hepplewhite and his contemporaries, is one of the most prominent of his motifs. The delicately pierced splat is of classic design with its scrolls and central ornament in the form of an inlaid medallion of painted satinwood, a feature favored by him and other designers of this period including the brothers Adam. The carved ears of wheat with pendent bell flowers are both forms of ornament very frequently used in this style. The daintily modelled legs, which are straight, square and tapered, as well as the contour of the seat with its serpentine swell, are characteristic of the later Hepplewhite influence.

Great attention was paid at this time to the supports connecting the chair back with the rear legs, these supports being gracefully carved above the plane of the upholstered seat.

The style of Hepplewhite was one of simplicity. Gracefulness of line and restrained ornamentation, whether carved or inlaid, make the chairs of this period exceedingly distinguished, and those of Hepplewhite particularly so.

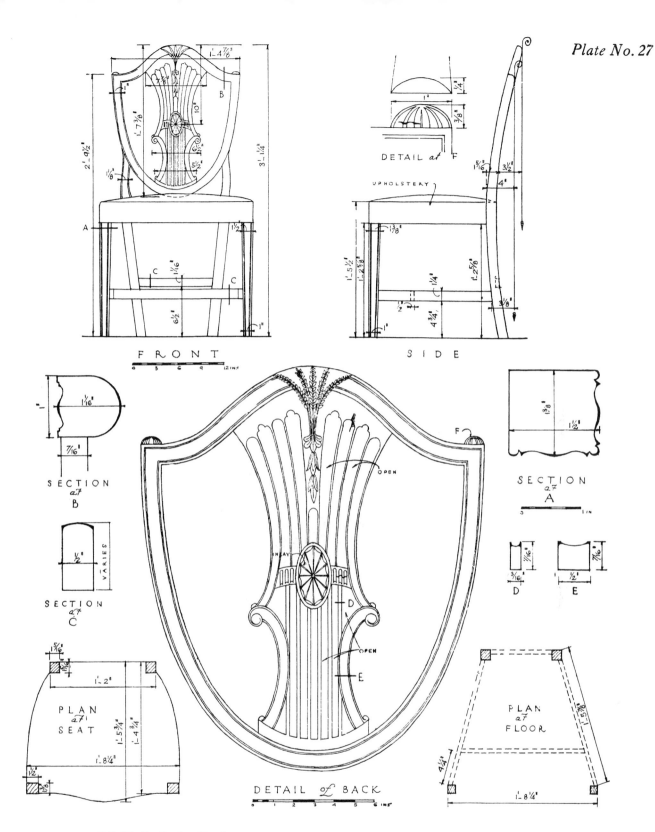

FRONT

SIDE

DETAIL at F

UPHOLSTERY

SECTION at B

SECTION at C

SECTION at A

D   E

PLAN at SEAT

DETAIL of BACK

PLAN at FLOOR

HEPPLEWHITE STYLE CHAIR
American about 1785-95 (Mahogany)
NOW IN THE METROPOLITAN MUSEUM OF ART

HEPPLEWHITE STYLE CHAIR

American 1785-1795

AN unusually elegant example of the shield back type of chair is that which is illustrated here. It is a product of American craftsmanship and shows a strong Hepplewhite influence. Hepplewhite rarely erred on the side of over-elaboration, and, although this example is handsomely carved, it is designed and executed with such restraint and daintiness and possesses such delicacy of outline that it is outstanding as one of the finest remaining specimens of this period produced in our colonies.

The legs are gracefully modeled on the lines of Louis Seize, the front ones being of taper form terminating in a thimble toe and with their two exposed faces enriched by the use of flutings.

Incorporated in the flare of the front seat frame and of use in the shaping of the rails is the serpentine curve. Of particular interest is the scheme of ornamentation contained within the back frame. Three splats rise from a carved and gilded motif, taking the form of conventional lilies from which issue streamers of grass and ears of wheat, and terminate on the top rail in a pierced and intertwining design.

Originally the entire framework was lacquered but has since been restored by gilding.

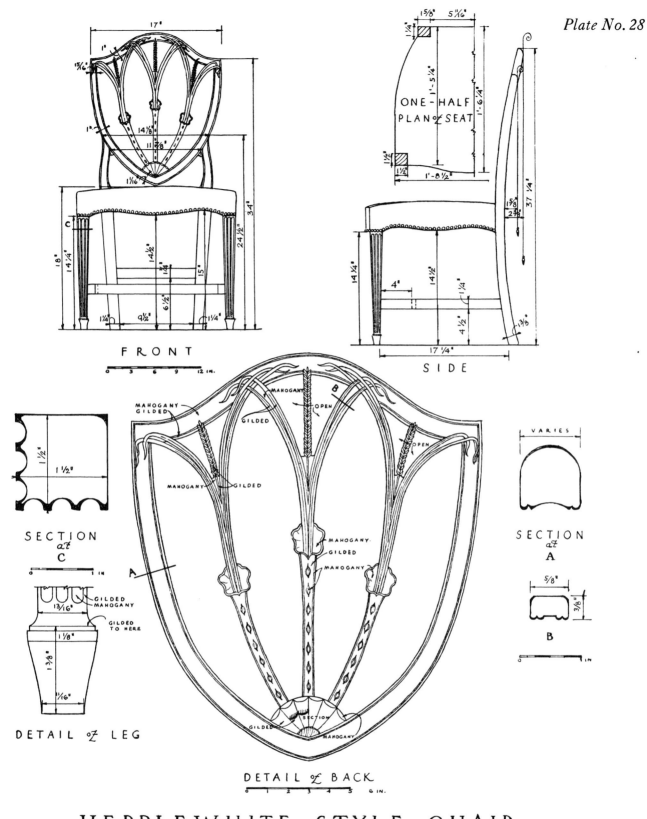

ONE-HALF
PLAN of SEAT

FRONT

SIDE

SECTION at C

DETAIL of LEG

SECTION at A

B

VARIES

DETAIL of BACK

MAHOGANY GILDED
MAHOGANY
OPEN
GILDED
MAHOGANY GILDED
OPEN
MAHOGANY
GILDED
MAHOGANY
GILDED
MAHOGANY

GILDED MAHOGANY
GILDED TO HERE

HEPPLEWHITE STYLE CHAIR
American about 1785-95 (Mahogany)
NOW IN THE PENDLETON COLLECTION · RHODE ISLAND SCHOOL OF DESIGN · PROVIDENCE R.I.

WINDOW SEAT, HEPPLEWHITE
English 1775-1800

GEORGE HEPPLEWHITE, originator of the style bearing his name as well as the business, which, after his death, was carried on by his widow Alice under the name of A. Hepplewhite & Company, devoted the greater part of his energies to the creation of small models of dainty and light proportions.

This window seat belongs to the later phase of the Hepplewhite style at the time when Hepplewhite was carrying out some of his major commissions, principally chairs, for the brothers Adam, the famous architects and designers.

Many authorities feel that Hepplewhite, although his knowledge of classical design was most limited, in carrying out the suggestions made by the "Adelphi," as the Adams were called, translated and incorporated them in his own creations in such a way that they frequently excelled, with their soft lines and charm of detail, those he patterned.

The gracefully curved line to which Hepplewhite was partial is in this window seat used in fashioning the rolled over upholstered arms. The seat and leg frame, in construction and in its rich but unostentatious ornamentation, shows plainly the Adelphi influences together with the grace and discrimination displayed by Hepplewhite.

Carved mahogany was used in the exposed framework of this charming piece of furniture.

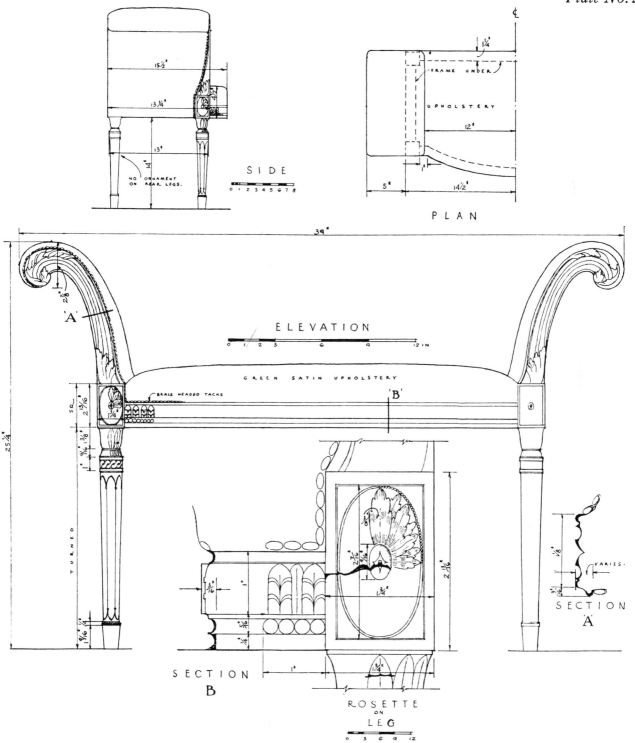

SIDE

PLAN

ELEVATION

GREEN SATIN UPHOLSTERY

BRASS HEADED TACKS

15½"

13¼"

13"

4"

NO ORNAMENT ON REAR LEGS.

0 1 2 3 4 5 6 7 8

FRAME UNDER

UPHOLSTERY

12"

5"

14½"

1¼"

1"

¢

39"

25¼"

2⅛"

'A'

SQ.

2⁵⁄₁₆

¼"

2"

⁹⁄₁₆ ³⁄₈

1"

TURNED

⁹⁄₁₆ ¼

0 1 2 3 6 9 12 IN

SECTION B

3⁄₁₆

1"

⁵⁄₈

¼

1"

'B'

2⁷⁄₁₆

1⁵⁄₁₆

2⅛"

1¼"

2¹⁄₁₆

SECTION 'A'

¹⁄₈"

VARIES.

³⁄₁₆

ROSETTE ON LEG

1¾"

0 3 6 9 12

WINDOW SEAT *Style of* HEPPLEWHITE
English 1775-1800 (Mahogany)
NOW IN THE METROPOLITAN MUSEUM OF ART

SETTEE, STYLE OF ADAM-HEPPLEWHITE

English 1770-1780

TO ROBERT and James Adam, architects and designers of the late 18th century in England, is attributed the crystallization of a style taking its inspiration from a revival of classicism in its more chaste form. Robert Adam studied the masterpieces of antiquity in Greece and Italy, bringing back to England in 1758 his knowledge and talent, which, combined with that of his brother James, gave a decided impetus to the then prevailing architectural trend.

Not cabinet makers themselves, the brothers Adam commissioned the Hepplewhites, Chippendales, Gillows and Seddons, and also others, to execute various pieces of furniture after their designs and to harmonize with the particular architectural settings they had created. On the other hand the cabinet makers mentioned above, designing contemporaneously and independently, caused a fusion of varying methods of treatment which resulted at times in such pieces of furniture as the mahogany settee shown here. Just which motifs or characteristics in this piece may be attributed to Hepplewhite, and which to the brothers Adam, is difficult to say, especially since it is known that they received inspiration from each other.

There is a decided likeness, in the tapering and fluted legs and in the oval carved medallions emphasizing each leg, to the Louis Seize style, then prevailing in France, and from which Hepplewhite also gracefully modeled his lines.

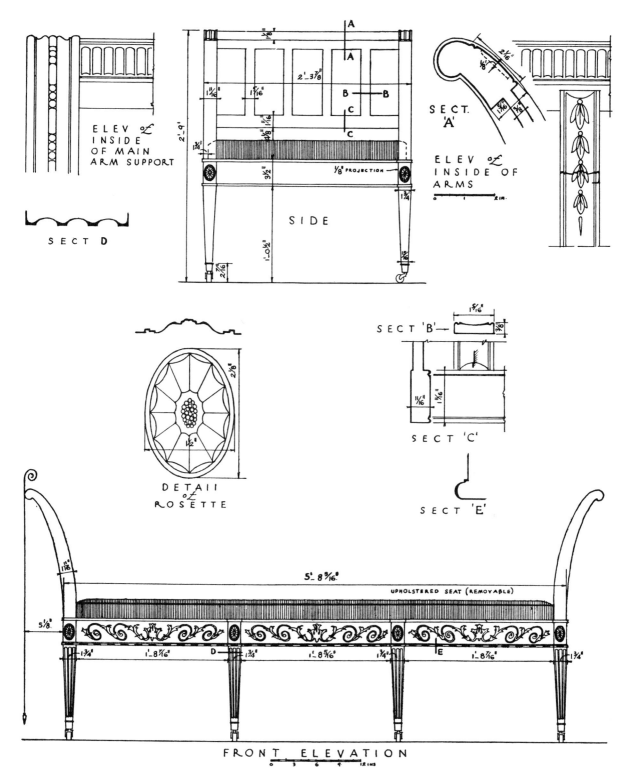

ELEV *of* INSIDE OF MAIN ARM SUPPORT

SECT D

SIDE

SECT 'A'

ELEV *of* INSIDE OF ARMS

SECT 'B'

SECT 'C'

SECT 'E'

DETAIL *of* ROSETTE

FRONT ELEVATION

UPHOLSTERED SEAT (REMOVABLE)

SETTEE *style of* ADAM-HEPPLEWHITE
English 1770-1780 (*Mahogany*)
NOW IN THE METROPOLITAN MUSEUM OF ART

SHERATON STYLE CHAIR
American 1790-1800

THIS chair executed in our Colonies, during the latter part of the Sheraton influence, exemplifies many of the prominent characteristics of this school of furniture design. Dignity and refinement, with stateliness and grace, mark the work of this period.

With the exception of the curved top rail, the framework of the back used at this time was square in shape. This curved top rail was not invariably, although frequently, the case. The filling at times consists of a panel, enclosing diagonal members of geometric severity, forming a lattice pattern and supported upon a bar raised above the seat line. The moulded latticed members are ornamented at their intersection by a leaf motif simply and delicately carved. Small carved rosettes mark the con-

nection of these diagonals at the top rail. The distribution of ornamentation under this influence is carefully balanced to give the impression of serenity and repose.

The seat is plain in straight design and tapered toward the rear with slightly rounded front and sides and is completely covered with upholstery which is held in place with brass headed nails. The legs are square, with moulded faces, and of taper form.

This design, severe in line and delicate in ornament, is of classical inspiration and is closely allied with the classic forms of the Renaissance which were so successfully interpreted in the Louis Seize style.

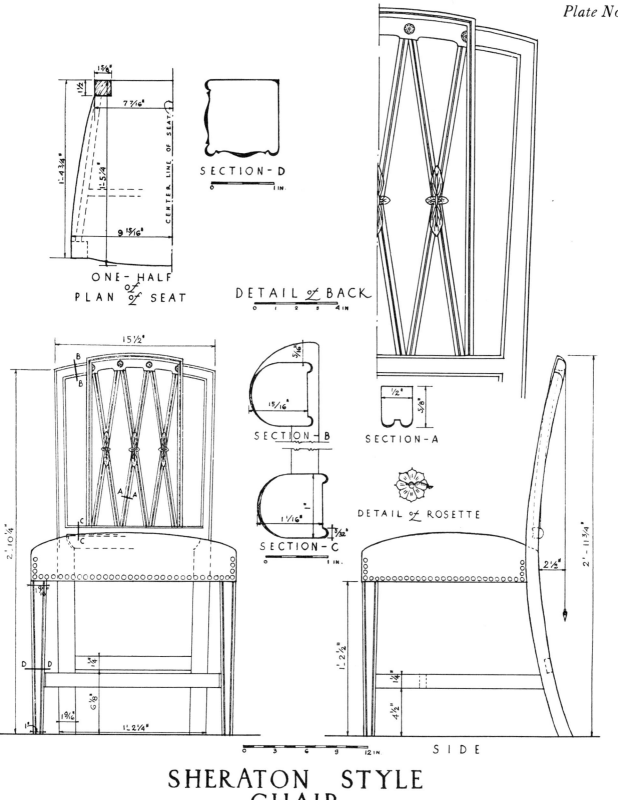

SECTION-D

ONE-HALF
of
PLAN *of* SEAT

DETAIL *of* BACK

SECTION-B

SECTION-A

SECTION-C

DETAIL *of* ROSETTE

SIDE

SHERATON STYLE
CHAIR
American 1790-1800 (Mahogany)
NOW IN THE ESSEX INSTITUTE SALEM MASS.

SHERATON STYLE CHAIR
American Late XVIII Century

ANOTHER specimen of a New England Sheraton side chair is this design which is contemporaneous with that shown on the preceding plate. These two examples resemble each other both in slender structural form and in general proportions. In this particular chair, however, the stretcher work at the legs has been omitted and the front of the seat kept straight, a method as characteristic of the more common usage among chairs of the Sheraton period as that employed in the chair preceding.

The top rail of the back frame is horizontal and relieved by a delicately carved cresting of conventionalized water leaves. Rosettes, inset, mark the intersections of the perpendicular and horizontal members of the back frame. Within this framework and supported upon the bottom rail—the use of the latter being an outstanding feature of Sheraton chairs—is a graceful design of curved members which give the effect of three openwork perpendicular splats which widen at their bases and at their tops.

Reeding was one of the characteristic methods of ornamentation of this style. It is here used on the face of all important members,—on the front legs, the back framework, and on the curved splat work, giving to the whole design a feeling of delicacy and attenuation.

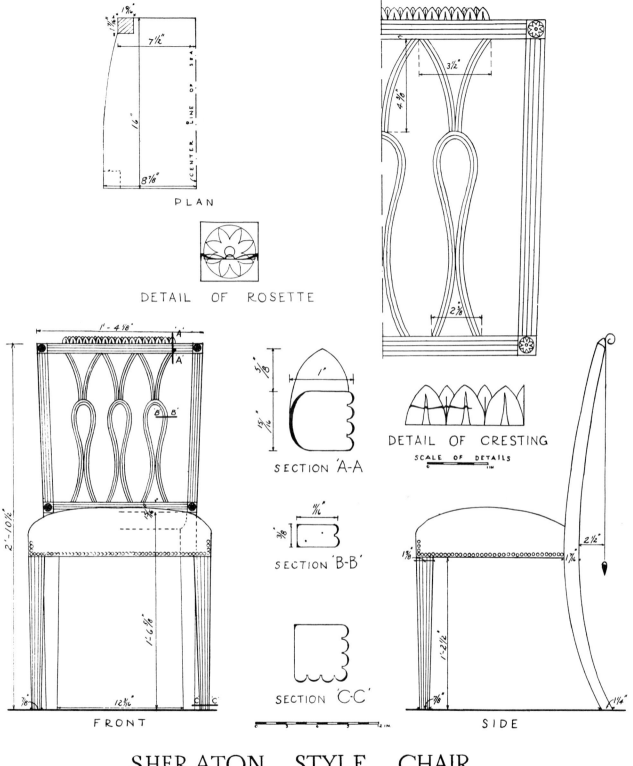

PLAN

DETAIL OF ROSETTE

SECTION 'A-A'

SECTION 'B-B'

SECTION 'C-C'

DETAIL OF CRESTING

SCALE OF DETAILS

FRONT

SIDE

SHERATON STYLE CHAIR
American Late 18th Century (Mahogany)
NOW IN THE ESSEX INSTITUTE, SALEM, MASS.

SHERATON STYLE CHAIR
American Late XVIII Century

NOT so distinctly characteristic of its Sheraton prototypes is this example of American extraction. It seems to exemplify to a marked degree the art of furniture designing executed by more or less unprejudiced American craftsmen; although it incorporates many of the major characteristics of this particular style in its square back frame, its square tapered legs, in the classical sources of its well placed ornamentation, the shaped plan of the chair seat, and above all in its design of virile dignity combined with delicate charm of line. American made chairs were, as a rule, sturdier than those of their English prototypes.

The perpendicular splats are delicately shaped and carved and are embraced within the back frame. The bases of these splats are widened at their tops and connected by a flaring motif, just below their juncture with the cresting rail. This widening surface is decorated with a water acanthus leaf carved in delicate relief. At the center of the cresting rail is incorporated an oblong plaque on which is carved a motif much used in the late 18th century in our country—the eagle with outstretched wings. As an emblem of decoration, this American bird came into vogue at the time of the inauguration of Washington.

The chair is more typical of the earlier phases of Sheraton influence when three or five splats were contained within the back frame. Also, the undecorated square and tapered leg are of the earlier date.

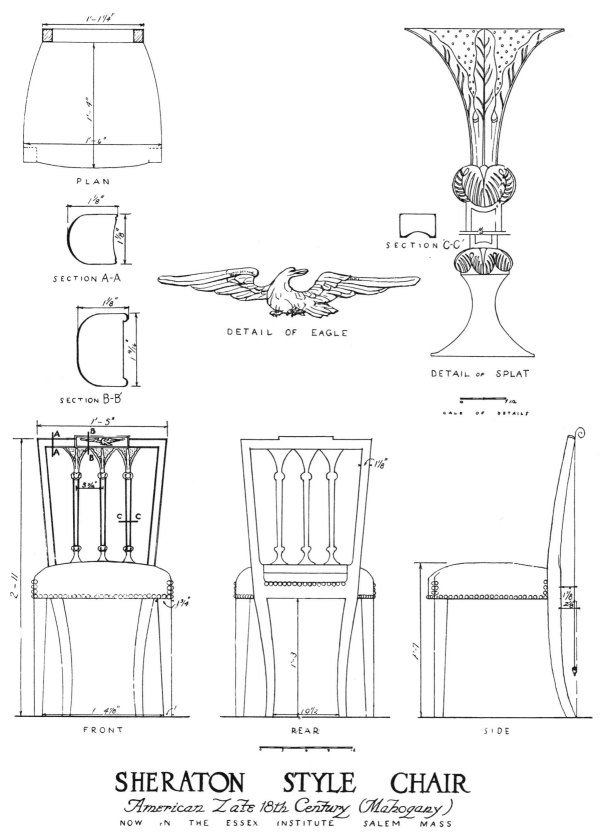

PLAN

SECTION A-A

SECTION B-B'

DETAIL OF EAGLE

SECTION C-C'

DETAIL OF SPLAT

SCALE OF DETAILS

FRONT

REAR

SIDE

SHERATON STYLE CHAIR

American Late 18th Century (Mahogany)

NOW IN THE ESSEX INSTITUTE SALEM MASS

SHERATON SETTEE

American 1790-1800

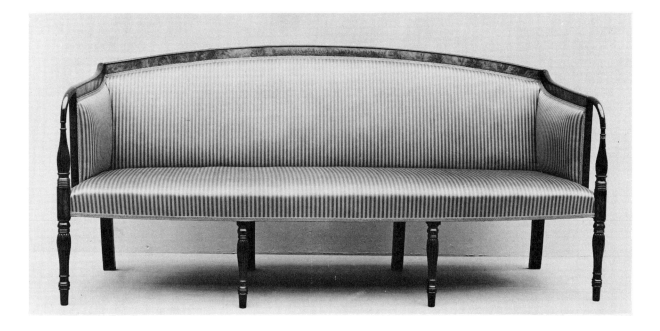

THE elegant settees made under the influence of the late Sheraton style are of delicate but strong construction. The exposed framework of the model here shown is of satinwood of an exceedingly decorative grain. The narrow band of wood which forms the back and arms follows subtle curves, (a form greatly favored by Sheraton.) The settee legs are straight and tapered with tasteful turnings and reeded ornamentation. The arm supports repeat the outline and decoration of the legs and are carried back to the solid arm with an easy curve. The legs, arm supports and band capping the framework are of rosewood. A band of satinwood inlay is inserted in the front legs at the height of the seat.

At the time that this settee was executed Sheraton introduced an intricate design of inlaid diagonal strips of wood, which appears in this particular piece of furniture in the vertical strips behind the arm supports. Very narrow bands of ebony and holly inlay border both sides of the back and arm framework immediately above the upholstery.

Delicacy and grace of modelling and mastery of line are predominating features of this Sheraton settee.

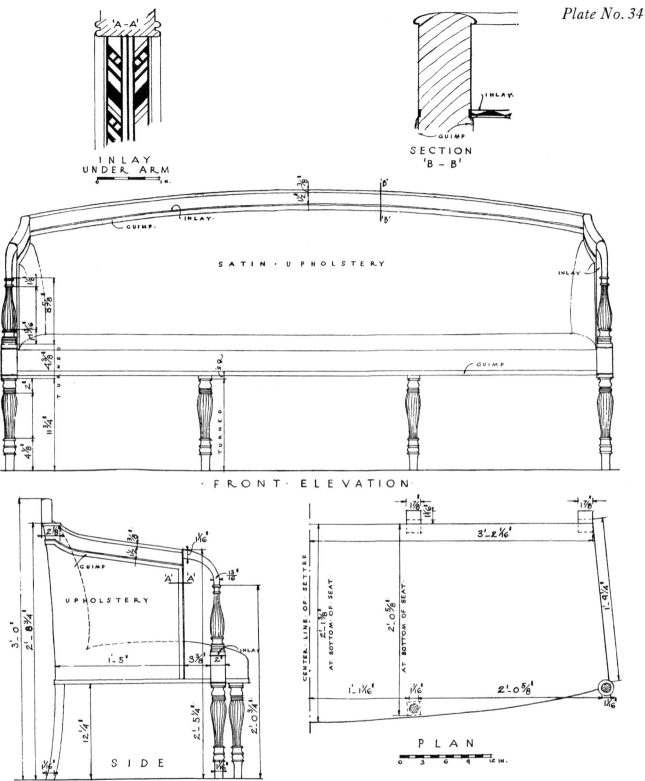

INLAY
UNDER ARM

SECTION
'B – B'

· FRONT· ELEVATION·

SIDE

PLAN

SHERATON SETTEE
American 1790–1800 (Satinwood Veneer)
NOW IN THE METROPOLITAN MUSEUM OF ART

SHERATON STYLE ARM CHAIR
English Late XVIII Century

THIS arm chair reflects to a marked degree the vogue, prevailing in the late 18th century in England, for composition and detail as applied to furniture. At this time Sheraton's most successful productions show the outgrowth of his collaboration with the brothers Adam who drew their inspiration in furniture designing directly from classical sources and from the then contemporaneous designs of France. At the height of his success, Sheraton interpreted these influences for the most part in a rather puritanical fashion by eliminating overdecoration and by giving to his designs a refining simplicity which, at times and through emphasis, produced an effect of severity.

The rectangular form of chair design with upholstered square back and seat frame is evidenced in this particular example. The Sheraton leg, of light construction in comparison with that which preceded, was almost invariably tapered and either square or round in section. In this chair the leg is decorated with an adaptation of a reeded pattern which culminates below the seat frame in carving more or less reminiscent of a capital motif. Carving also enriches the framework proper with a running bead ornament and with carved rosettes, emphasizing the intersections of its various members.

The partially cushioned arms resting upon supports fashioned in vase form and carved in a spiral design rise from the side of the seat frame and sweep upward to the height of the back. Carving, similar to that which decorates the back and seat frames, is also applied to the top surface of these curving arms.

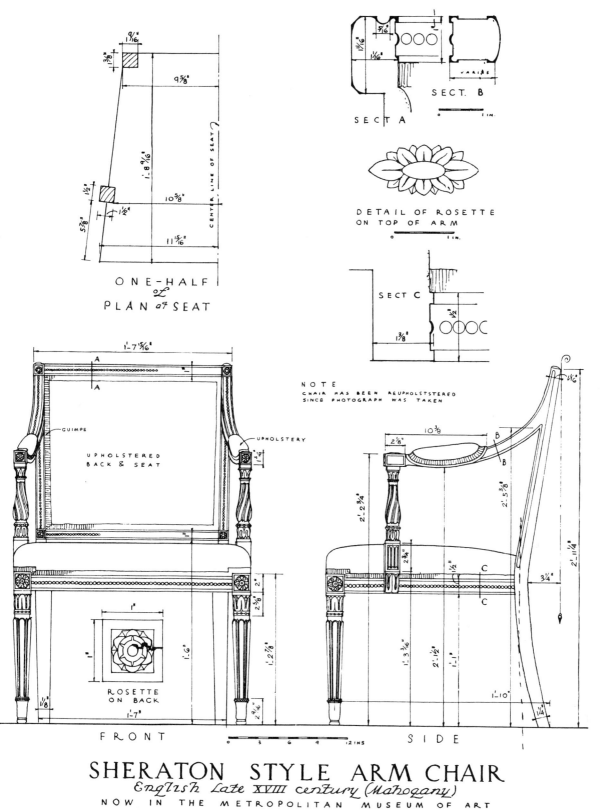

ONE-HALF
of
PLAN *of* SEAT

SECT. A

SECT. B

DETAIL OF ROSETTE
ON TOP OF ARM

SECT C

NOTE
CHAIR HAS BEEN REUPHOLSTERED
SINCE PHOTOGRAPH WAS TAKEN

GUIMPE

UPHOLSTERY

UPHOLSTERED
BACK & SEAT

ROSETTE
ON BACK

FRONT

SIDE

SHERATON STYLE ARM CHAIR
English Late XVIII century (Mahogany)
NOW IN THE METROPOLITAN MUSEUM OF ART

ITALIAN SETTEE

Eighteenth Century

AN adaptation of the lyre-back chair motif, delightful in its design, is incorporated in this 18th century Italian settee. It is representative of the finest furniture produced in Italy during that century.

This particular pattern, that of the lyre, probably originated with the brothers Adam who in turn borrowed it from classic sources. In other respects, as well, this piece of furniture is closely patterned after the designs of contemporary English cabinet makers.

The construction is rectilinear and exceedingly graceful, showing outlines relieved by well placed detail which has been executed in a restrained and delicate fashion. The legs, as well as the straight back supports, are square and tapered with their exposed faces ornamented with flutings. These straight supports, however, are of the inverted form of those forming the legs. The seat alone is upholstered.

The body of the settee is painted in greyish green while the fillets, ornaments and flutings are gilded, producing a richly contrasting effect, in full accord with the general style of the piece.

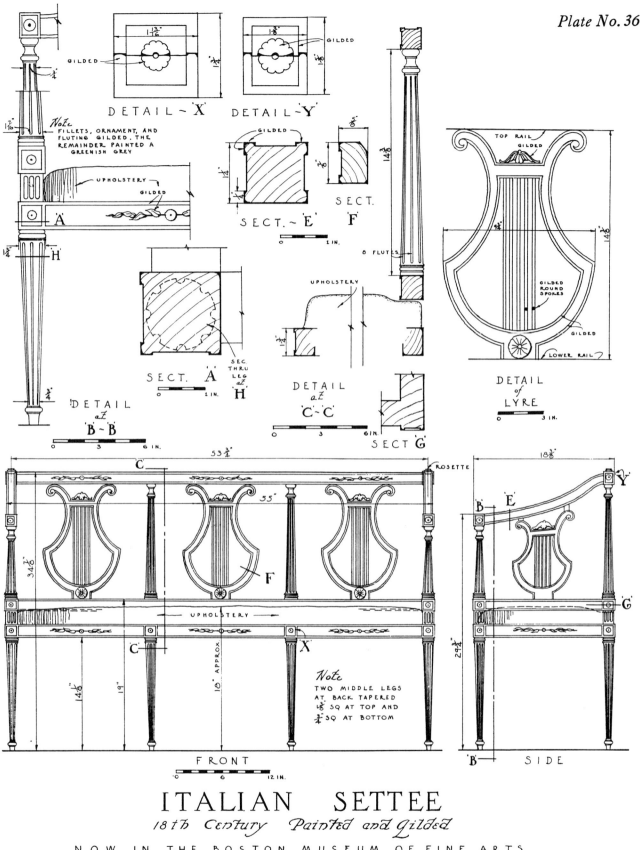

ITALIAN SETTEE
18th Century Painted and Gilded

NOW IN THE BOSTON MUSEUM OF FINE ARTS

DUNCAN PHYFE ARM CHAIR
American 1800-1815

THE furniture which was produced in the workshop of the American designer, Duncan Phyfe, although he created a style of his own, may be classed according to the influence under which it fell. The accompanying chair comes under the first group with Hepplewhite and Sheraton influence predominating. This phase gave way to one in which the Directoire, combined with English forms and details, held sway, which in turn was supplanted by the third, that of the full Empire style.

In this chair the rectangular framework of the back with its latticed cross-bars, the cylindrical legs with shaped endings at the feet, and the reeding, consistently used throughout as a medium of enriching the flat surfaces, indicate the influence of the Sheraton vogue. More peculiar to the designs of Duncan Phyfe are the seat in the shape of a horse-shoe with the broad rail reeded, the dished top rail with its paneling of reed work and the relation of the arm extended to the seat with the leg beneath. In Sheraton examples legwork was generally prolonged to form supports for the gracefully curving arms.

The work of Duncan Phyfe forms a link between that era of good design sponsored by Hepplewhite and Sheraton and the succeeding period of questionable taste.

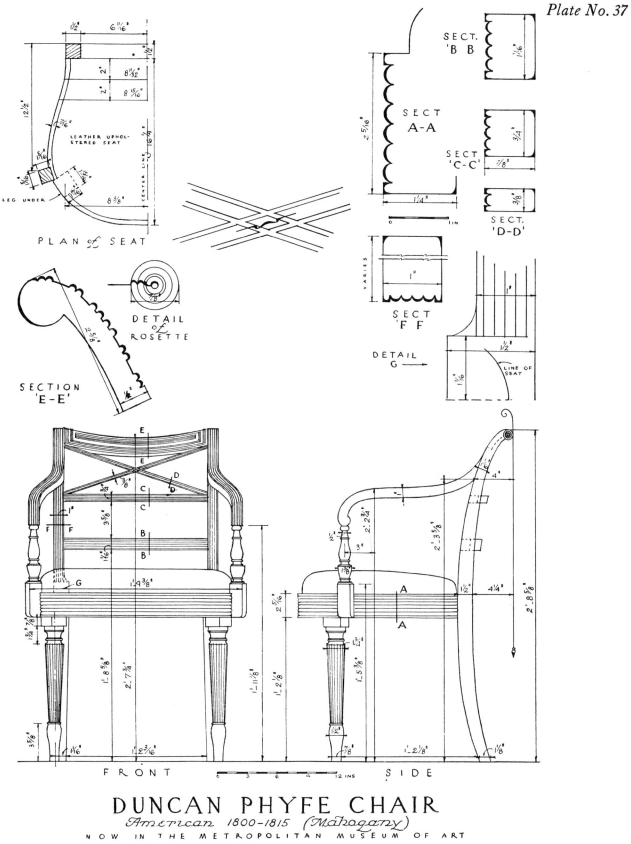

SECT.
'B B'

SECT
A-A

SECT
'C-C'

SECT.
'D-D'

SECT
'F F'

DETAIL
G

LINE OF
SEAT

PLAN of SEAT

LEATHER UPHOL-
STERED SEAT

CENTER LINE

LEG UNDER

DETAIL
of
ROSETTE

SECTION
'E-E'

FRONT

SIDE

DUNCAN PHYFE CHAIR
American 1800-1815 (Mahogany)
NOW IN THE METROPOLITAN MUSEUM OF ART

LYRE BACK DUNCAN PHYFE CHAIR
American Early XIX Century

THIS lyre-back side chair typifies the Directoire phase of the Duncan Phyfe chair designs. At this time, the first years of the 19th century, a taste for French designs became popular in New York City, and Phyfe, accordingly, adopted and combined with the prevailing English forms and motifs certain elements of the styles of furniture then in vogue in France.

The legs of this example form reversed curves with the faces of those in front decorated with the conventionalized acanthus leaf carved in low relief. A delicately carved lyre, forming a short splat, is embraced within the framework of the gracefully sweeping back. The brass strings of the lyre used in this chair were frequently substituted for those of whalebone. The carved acanthus leaf, so individually characteristic of Duncan Phyfe's designs, is also used to enrich the scrolls of the lyre.

Duncan Phyfe was an apostle of excellent workmanship and a designer of discriminating taste, choosing and placing his ornamentation with the greatest discretion. He displayed great care in the selection of mahogany used, both as to graining and color.

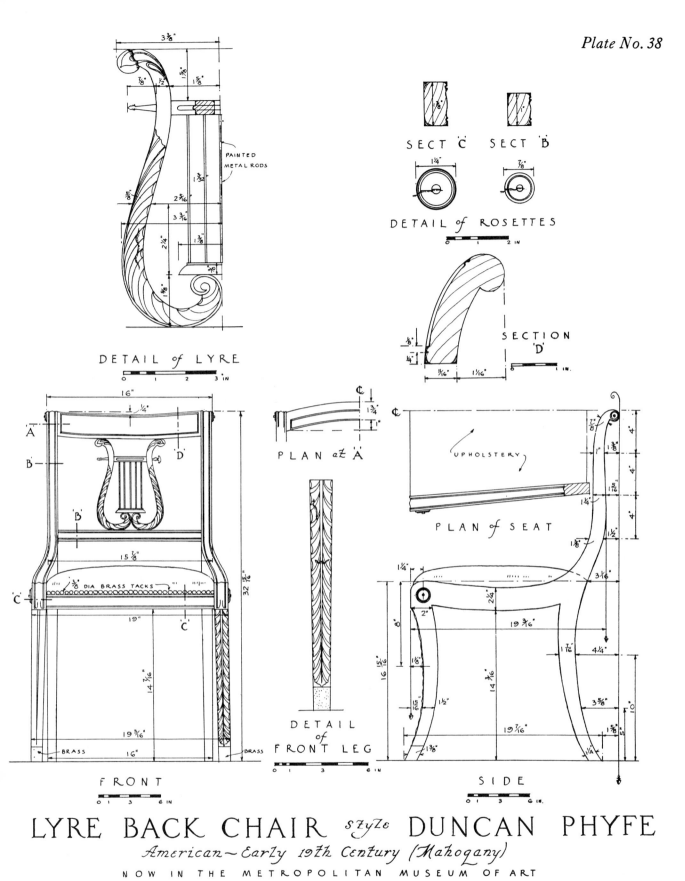

DETAIL of LYRE

SECT C SECT B

DETAIL of ROSETTES

SECTION 'D'

PLAN at A

PLAN of SEAT

FRONT

DETAIL of FRONT LEG

SIDE

UPHOLSTERY

PAINTED METAL RODS

DIA BRASS TACKS

BRASS

LYRE BACK CHAIR *Style* DUNCAN PHYFE

American ~ Early 19th Century (Mahogany)

NOW IN THE METROPOLITAN MUSEUM OF ART

ITALIAN TABLE
XVI Century

AS explained before in the discussion of an Italian chair, the pronounced characteristics of the furniture of the Italian Renaissance are stateliness and formality, execution on a bold and robust scale and a strong architectural influence. Adaptations of classic Greek and Roman motifs comprised the ornamentation.

Among those motifs most favored was the acanthus leaf and scroll which has been applied to ornament the leg supports of the accompanying table. In this instance, the scroll shapes the knees of the legs and flows into the acanthus leaf, boldly carved, which terminates in large lion's paws. The anthemion, also a design from classical sources, decorates the juncture of the legs.

Above the knee scrolls, the horizontal top member of the legs is moulded and flares outward in cyma curves to support the table top whose exposed edges are also moulded in accordance with the contours preferred at this time.

A stretcher with chamfered edges, placed close to the table top, ties together the supporting leg members. This horizontal tie runs through and projects beyond the supports where it is held rigid by means of wooden pegs.

The wood in this·example is walnut which was the material chiefly employed during the period of the Renaissance in Italy.

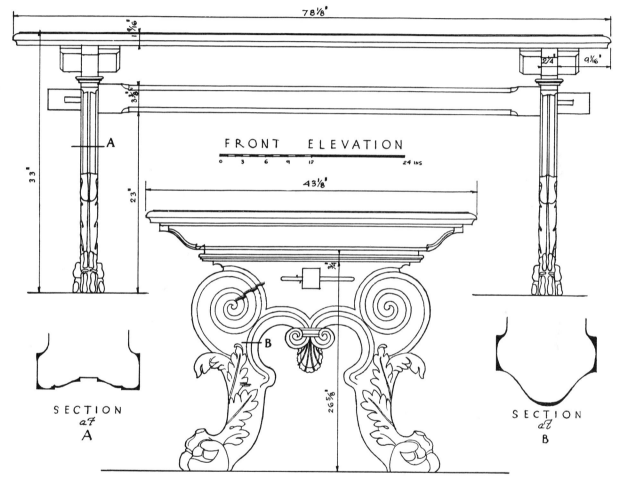

78⅛"

1⁹⁄₁₆"

2¼" 9¹⁄₁₆"

3⅜"

A

FRONT ELEVATION

0 3 6 9 12 24 INS

43⅛"

33"

23"

¾"

B

26⅝"

SECTION
at
A

SECTION
at
B

SIDE

ITALIAN TABLE
XVI Century (Walnut)
NOW IN THE METROPOLITAN MUSEUM OF ART

OAK TABLE
English XVII Century

THE furniture of the Jacobean period was staunch and simple of structure and executed with vigor and was quite expressive of the manners and temperament of the English people during the 17th century.

This refectory table shows some of the familiar characteristics of that period; sturdy cylindrical turnings of the legs, firmly braced by heavy stretchers; rather massive structure; long, narrow proportions of the table top built upon the traditional lines of the trestle table; and the unusual type of carving favored at that time—which in this case is confined to one long face of the moulded apron. Of

particular interest is the difference in the size of the front and rear legs, those in front being less massive than those in the rear.

Oak was the wood in general use at that time. Its durability, weight and strength made it a favorite for the execution of these simple, heavy designs.

Carving of a bold and rugged type has been used with restraint on this particular table. The "scratch" carving on the central flat band of the ornamental surface is of a geometric design, while the ovolo mouldings bordering this band are of a pattern of simple foliage, incised or "gouged" sharply from the surface of the wood.

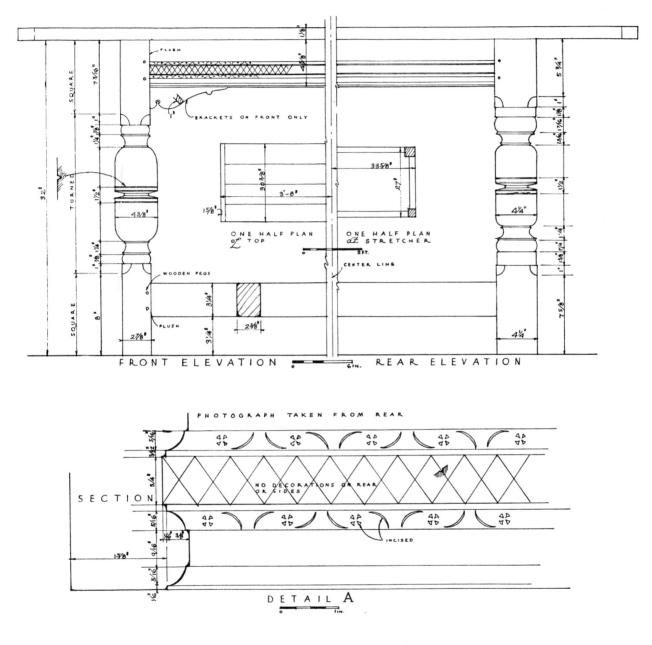

FRONT ELEVATION   REAR ELEVATION

ONE HALF PLAN OF TOP

ONE HALF PLAN OF STRETCHER

CENTER LINE

SECTION

PHOTOGRAPH TAKEN FROM REAR

NO DECORATIONS ON REAR OR SIDES

INCISED

DETAIL A

OAK TABLE
English Seventeenth Century
NOW IN THE METROPOLITAN MUSEUM OF ART

OAK BENCH

English XVII Century

STOOLS and benches were decidedly popular during the Jacobean period. The cabinet makers of that time turned them out in great quantities. The functions they were called upon to fulfill were varied. Sometimes they were used as small tables, again as occasional seats, and quite often, they were placed at the end of long tables. They took the place of chairs, which were then only just coming into vogue in England, and, in addition, carried on in a limited manner the duties we now place upon a variety of small tables.

They were sturdily built, appearing usually with turned legs which were, as in the accompanying example, splayed to insure greater stability. The turnings of the legs of this specimen, which are of stolid proportions, are of the ring baluster type.

They are held rigidly in place by means of heavy aprons and stretchers, richly moulded.

An ornamental floral band of Renaissance design is carved upon the deep front apron of this stool, carving being a favorite method of decorative expression of Jacobean furniture. This carving is of the "modeled" type, standing out in bold relief from a lowered surface.

A decorative effect, produced by the use of inlaid woods, was also then in fashion and is here applied to the flat bands of floor stretchers and to the rear and side of the aprons in an effective geometric pattern. Bone, ivory, mother-of-pearl and tortoise shell were also effectively used, in striking patterns of inlay, upon benches of the period.

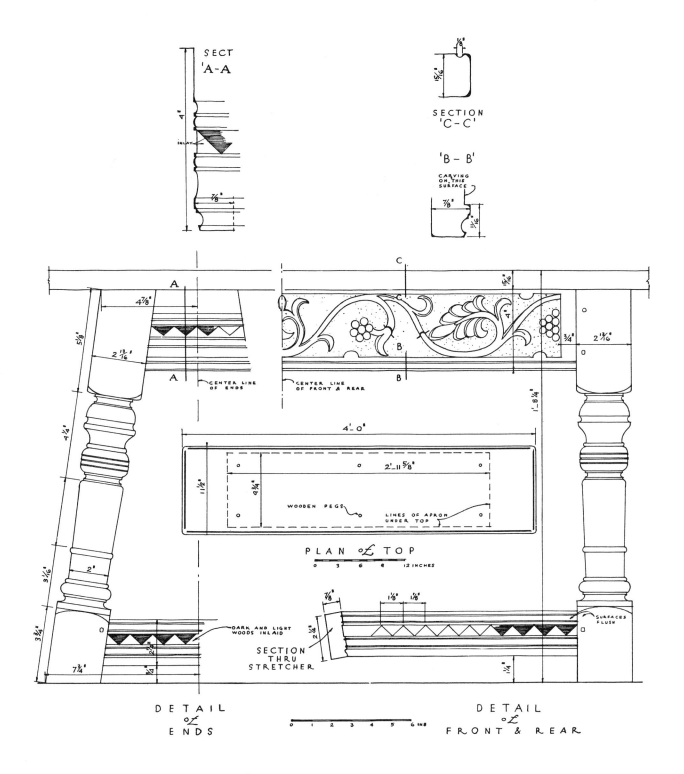

SECT
'A-A'

4"

INLAY

7/8"

SECTION
'C-C'

'B-B'

CARVING ON THIS SURFACE

7/8"

1/16"

A — A

4 7/8"

2 13/16"

CENTER LINE OF ENDS

CENTER LINE OF FRONT & REAR

C

B — B

4"

3/4"

2 13/16"

1'-8 1/4"

5/8"

4 1/4"

3 1/16"

2"

3 3/4"

7 3/4"

4'-0"

2'-11 5/8"

1 1/2"

9 3/4"

WOODEN PEGS

LINES OF APRON UNDER TOP

PLAN OF TOP

0 3 6 9 12 INCHES

7/8"

1 1/8" 1 1/8"

DARK AND LIGHT WOODS INLAID

2 1/8"

SECTION THRU STRETCHER

SURFACES FLUSH

1/4"

DETAIL OF ENDS

0 1 2 3 4 5 6 INS

DETAIL OF FRONT & REAR

OAK BENCH
English Seventeenth Century

FLEMISH TABLE
XVII Century

IN FLEMISH furniture, during the 17th century, carved supports representing figures gradually gave way to those of turned or twisted shape. Those of spiral form, particularly, played an important role in the decorative scheme of the furniture of this time.

In this representative piece, the two end legs are joined by short floor stretchers partially twisted. The long central stretcher, connecting these coupled supports, carries at its center a turned vase ornament—a characteristic feature of the Dutch, Flemish and French furniture of the second half of the 17th century. It occurred on practically every piece of this period which stood upon four legs.

Rich carving was a much used form of decoration and here appears upon the blocks of the front leg supports, as well as upon the center stretcher block, below the vase shaped ornament, and upon the upper face of the end stretchers.

The lower edge of the apron is cut in a waving pattern. In the front apron is fitted a long drawer slightly projecting from the framework and operated by a wooden knob. The edge of the substantial top is handsomely moulded.

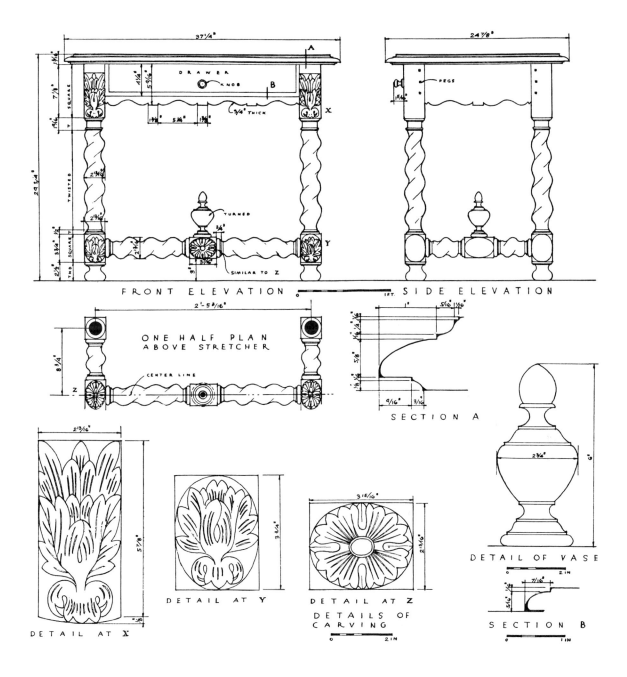

FRONT ELEVATION   SIDE ELEVATION

ONE HALF PLAN ABOVE STRETCHER

CENTER LINE

SECTION A

DETAIL AT X

DETAIL AT Y

DETAIL AT Z

DETAILS OF CARVING

DETAIL OF VASE

SECTION B

FLEMISH TABLE
17th Century (Walnut)

MAPLE TABLE

American 1700-1710

SMALL tables of various shapes became of general use about the close of the 17th century in England, due largely to the new custom of tea and coffee drinking and to the increase in popularity of cards and other games. In America, the types and designs of these small tables, as well as other articles of furniture, were patterned after the existing preferences and vogues of Europe, modified and interpreted to agree with the mannerisms and predilections of the colonists of the locality in which the furniture was executed.

Early 18th century tables made by our craftsmen show a severity and simplicity of line and are staunchly constructed. These joiners used many native woods, among them being oak and walnut for the finest work and maple, pine, cedar, elm, birch, cherry and ash for the general run.

This small oval-topped maple table is provided with four legs, splayed outward and turned. in baluster-shaped profiles of rather slender type. Below the table top the legs are connected with skirtings shaped in graceful cut-out patterns in a series of cyma curves, with those at the sides differing from those at the front and back faces. The floor stretchers are plain with rounded tops.

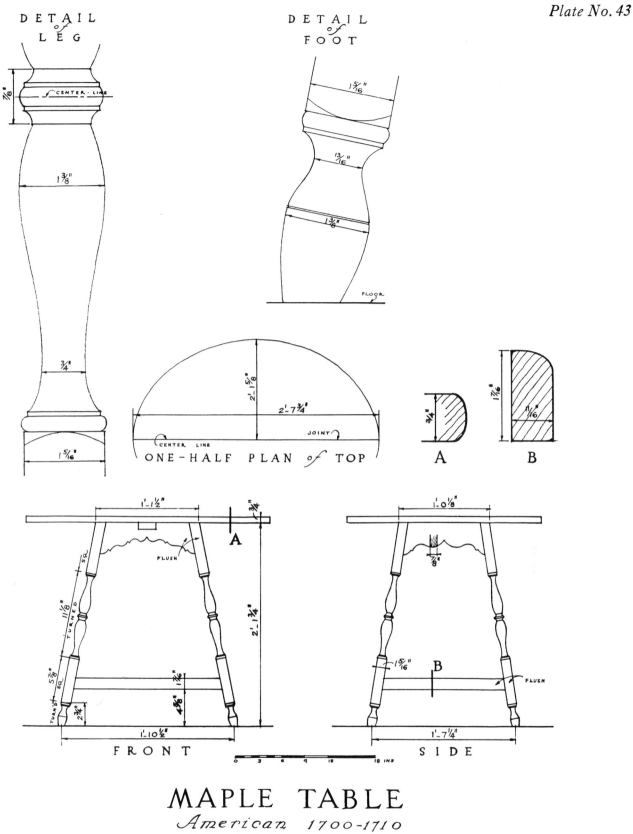

DETAIL
of
LEG

DETAIL
of
FOOT

ONE-HALF PLAN of TOP

A

B

FRONT

SIDE

MAPLE TABLE
American 1700-1710
NOW · IN · THE · METROPOLITAN · MUSEUM · OF · ART

TILT-TOP TABLE

American 1700

THE gate-leg table was very popular in the colonies during the last half of the 17th century and the first half of the 18th. The tilt-top table here shown, or folding-table, as it was sometimes called, is the gate-leg type. It is constructed with two leg-frames, one of which swings and folds against the other. The top is fastened with hinges to the fixed frame and drops into a vertical position when the gate swings. In a folded position the table cannot stand. The gate and top swing on metal pivots concealed in the uprights and stretchers.

The sturdy turnings of the legs and the round Dutch feet would seem to indicate Dutch influence.

At this time there was comparatively little difference between the furniture designs and construction of the Dutch and English colonists. Among the Dutch were excellent artisans and it was in a large measure due to them that their craftsmanship was infused into the then prevailing style.

The wood is maple, which has been stained to represent mahogany and given a waxed finish.

This simple table was evidently designed for utility, as it practically takes up no room when folded and yet presents a comparatively roomy top when extended.

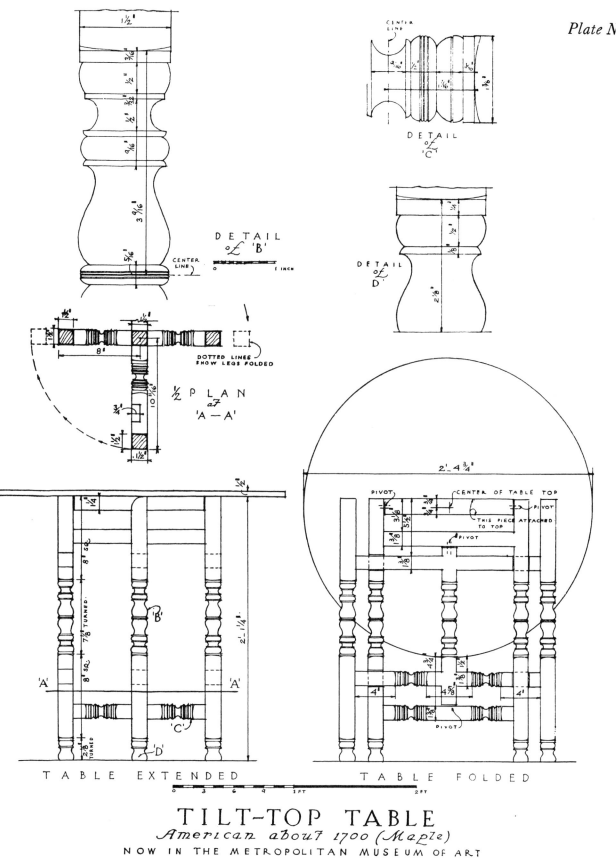

DETAIL of 'B'

DETAIL of 'C'

DETAIL of 'D'

CENTER LINE

DOTTED LINES SHOW LEGS FOLDED

½ PLAN at 'A — A'

PIVOT

CENTER OF TABLE TOP

THIS PIECE ATTACHED TO TOP

PIVOT

TABLE EXTENDED

TABLE FOLDED

TILT-TOP TABLE
American about 1700 (Maple)
NOW IN THE METROPOLITAN MUSEUM OF ART

BUTTERFLY TABLE

American 1700

THIS well designed and naive example of the Butterfly table is of early American craftsmanship, showing in its ample strength and sturdy lines both the Dutch and English influence. The slender legs are slightly raked and are gracefully turned in the baluster pattern. Plain stretchers, rounded at the top, brace the legs near the floor, and in the center of the longer stretchers are pivoted the large wings, whose flaring form gave the name of "Butterfly" to this type of table. The oval top is divided into three sections, the fixed central portion and the two ends which form drop leaves which are supported, when extended, upon the outspread wings. When closed these wings, which are also pivoted to the overhang of the table top, swing against the framework and allow the leaves to cover them.

This table is provided with one drawer running the full depth of the horizontal apron. A small thumb mould borders the drawer face and overlaps the frame. A wooden knob serves as drawer pull.

The wood from which this table is fashioned is maple, left unfinished. This table is unusually low, measuring only a little over two feet from floor to table top.

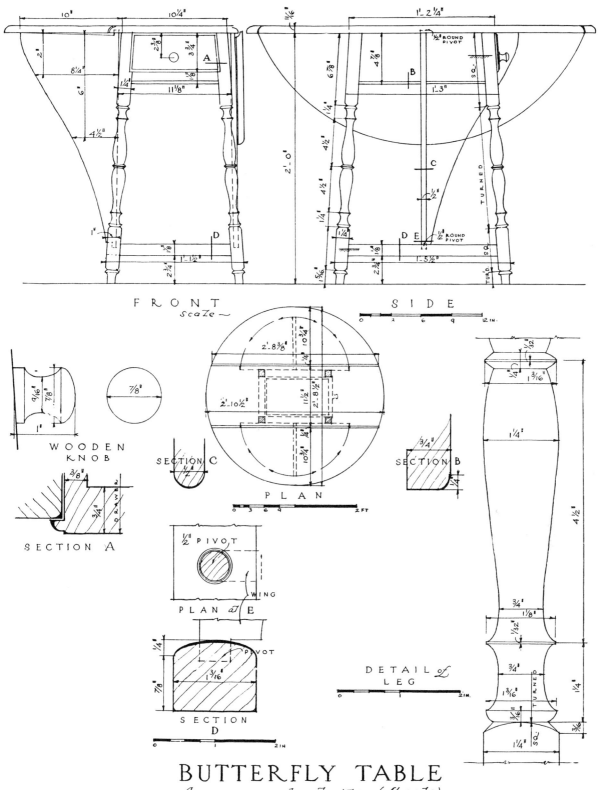

FRONT
scale

SIDE
0 3 6 9 12 IN.

WOODEN
KNOB

SECTION A

SECTION C

PLAN
0 3 6 ... 2 FT

SECTION B

DETAIL of
LEG
0 ... 2 IN.

PLAN at E

SECTION
D
0 ... 1 ... 2 IN.

BUTTERFLY TABLE
American about 1700 (Maple)
NOW IN THE METROPOLITAN MUSEUM OF ART

DROP LEAF TABLE

American About 1750

THIS drop-leaf table constructed in tripod form is a quaint and uncommon type. The top is supported upon a turned frame consisting of three legs and strengthened with straight, moulded stretchers. When extended, the top is round with those portions, overlapping the underlying apron, made into flaps, leaving a triangular center, and, when lowered, the flaps fit against the leg structure. This top is cleverly constructed to turn on a pivot placed in the center of the table top, so that the leaves may be supported by the corners of the framework below.

The lightening of the structure is characteristic of the late date which produced this particular specimen. The legs and feet are of the baluster type of turning and of rather delicate execution. A small bead moulding softens the lower edge of the apron framework.

Of American execution, this table was made of mahogany, differing from the usual custom among the colonial craftsmen of fashioning such small tables of this date from woods of a lighter color.

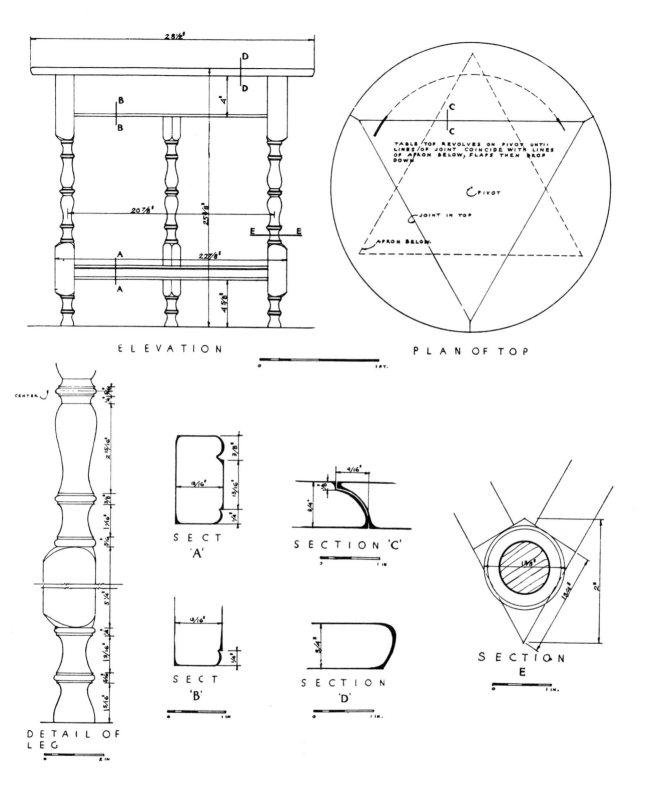

ELEVATION

PLAN OF TOP

TABLE TOP REVOLVES ON PIVOT UNTIL LINES OF JOINT COINCIDE WITH LINES OF APRON BELOW, FLAPS THEN DROP DOWN

PIVOT

JOINT IN TOP

APRON BELOW.

DETAIL OF LEG

SECT 'A'

SECT 'B'

SECTION 'C'

SECTION 'D'

SECTION E

DROP LEAF TABLE
American about 1750 (Mahogany)

TRIPOD TABLE
English 1755-1770

THE handsomest of the tripod tables were made about 1750 in England in the style of Chippendale. Mahogany was the popular wood of this time and the wood from which the accompanying example is made. The shaft, a cluster of columns quatrefoil in plan, is supported upon a bulbous form which rests upon three cabriole legs. Carving has been restricted in this table to the knee of the leg, where it appears in anglicized French character, and to the main swell of the shaft support and to the scalloped edge of the table top.

The character of the raised moulded rim of the latter gives to these tables the name of "Pie-crust."

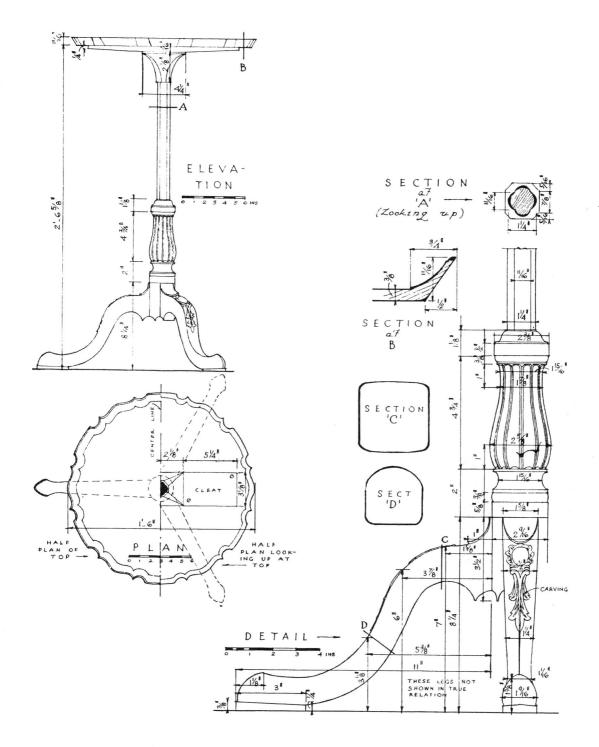

ELEVATION

0 1 2 3 4 5 6 INS

SECTION
at
'A'
(Looking up)

SECTION
at
B

SECTION
'C'

SECT
'D'

PLAN

HALF
PLAN OF
TOP →

← HALF
PLAN LOOK-
ING UP AT
TOP

0 1 2 3 4 5 6

CENTER LINE

CLEAT

DETAIL →

0 1 2 3 4 INS

CARVING

THESE LEGS NOT
SHOWN IN TRUE
RELATION

TRIPOD TABLE
Pie-crust Rim
CHIPPENDALE STYLE
English 1753-70 (Mahogany)

QUEEN ANNE STOOL

English About 1710

THIS stool, made during the reign of Queen Anne, is of walnut, the wood almost exclusively used during this period. The undulating lines of the cabriole legs, a feature introduced under this regime, is here used with the greatest simplicity, which, together with the lack of ornamentation shows off the beauty and figures of the wood. The gracefully curved legs terminate in round Dutch feet.

The seat is built upon a separate removable frame, upholstered in needlepoint of a bold, all-over pattern, of red and blue flowers on a buff field.

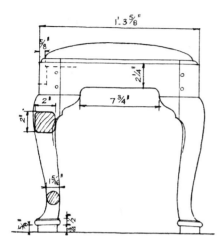

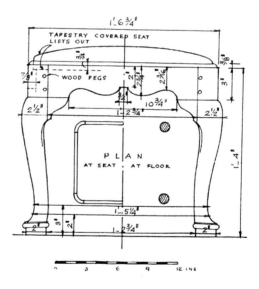

1'.6¾"

TAPESTRY COVERED SEAT
LIFTS OUT

WOOD PEGS

P L A N
AT SEAT : AT FLOOR

QUEEN ANNE
STOOL
English about 1710
(Walnut)

CARD TABLE
American, Dutch Influence

GAMING and card playing were favorite diversions during the 17th and 18th centuries, which prompted the execution of various small tables for these purposes. At the time, when Chippendale designs were followed, they were made in great numbers and appeared in several forms. One of the most usual types is that of the double top supported upon cabriole legs. The table illustrated follows these lines.

One of the rear legs is made to swing out in order to support the flap top when opened. The top is broken-fronted, with projecting square corners—before 1730 the corners were, for the most part, rounded—which, when open, discloses four dished compartments made for the purpose of holding candlesticks and also four oval-shaped wells for holding money or counters. These features were inherited from the time of Queen Anne.

This table is of the ornamental type of card table, with fretwork introduced on the slightly rounded edges of the top and with the frieze or apron below enriched by gracefully shaped panels, outlined with two connected rows of delicate beading. The lower edge of the rail, bracing the leg, is carved, as is likewise the bracket of the leg. Upon the knee is carved in relief a large shell with flower pendent—a common decoration of the Dutch period. The foot is an excellent example of the claw-and-ball type.

In England the earliest type of table especially designed for the playing of cards appeared about the close of the 17th century and remained in vogue until the end of the 18th when an attempt to suppress gambling was made.

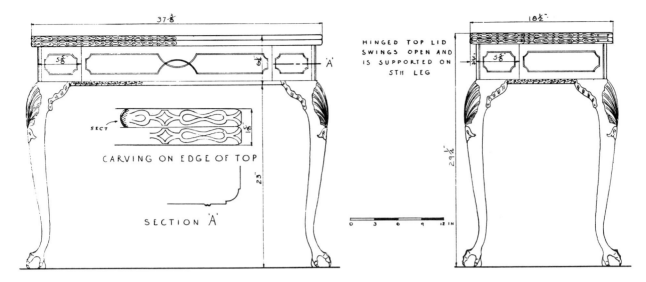

FRONT

SIDE

HINGED TOP LID
SWINGS OPEN AND
IS SUPPORTED ON
5TH LEG

CARVING ON EDGE OF TOP

SECTION "A"

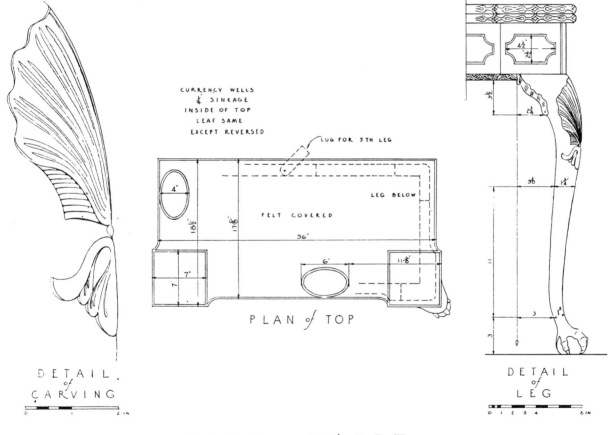

DETAIL
of
CARVING

CURRENCY WELLS
¼ SINKAGE
INSIDE OF TOP
LEAF SAME
EXCEPT REVERSED

LUG FOR 5TH LEG

LEG BELOW

FELT COVERED

PLAN of TOP

DETAIL
of
LEG

CARD TABLE
American, Dutch Influence, First Half 18th Century

NOW IN THE MUSEUM OF RHODE ISLAND SCHOOL OF DESIGN

CHAMBER DRESSING TABLE
American 1775-1800

DRESSING tables continued in vogue in England from the 17th century when they were first considered necessary articles of fashionable furniture.

This American-made dressing table is of the general proportions and construction of the type favored by Chippendale. Richly decorated, it shows the appropriation of motifs and manner of carving of the style of Louis Quinze, treated in a restrained and anglicized, yet bold, manner. The recessed shell and flamboyant foliage of the French school, adapted in a manner peculiar to Chippendale, are inserted and fill the large square of the lower central drawer. The skirt is richly scrolled, with a suggestion of rococo influence in its tracery, and embraces, at the center of the front, a boldly carved convex shell.

The cabriole leg with claw-and-ball foot is indicative of the school of Chippendale and is ornamented with a motif of acanthus leaves, freely carved. Classic colonettes, with fluted shafts, are recessed into the corners of the body carcase.

The long top drawers and the two flanking lower drawers are equipped with brass handles and escutcheons of an intricate pierced pattern. The small brass drop handle of the central lower drawer is applied to a carved leaf motif in the center of the convex shell.

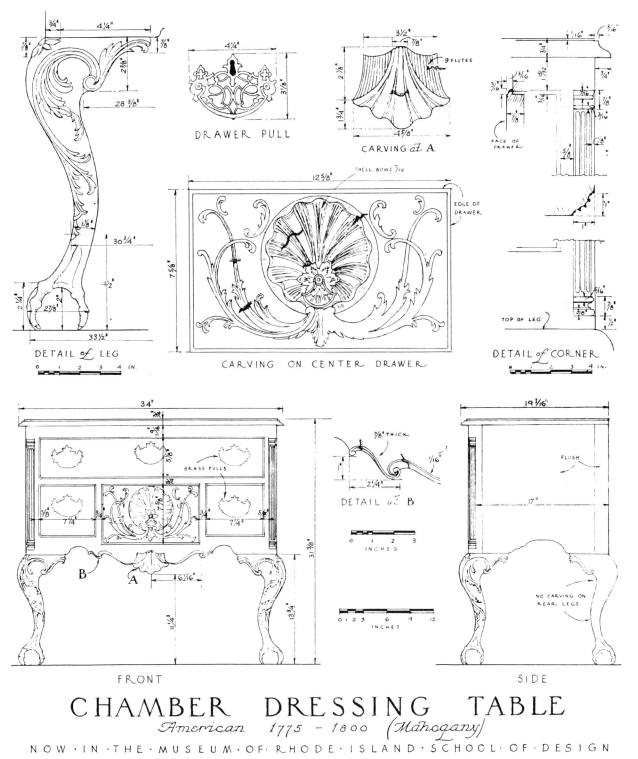

DRAWER PULL

CARVING at A

9 FLUTES

FACE OF DRAWER

SHELL BOWS 7/16

EDGE OF DRAWER

DETAIL of CORNER

TOP OF LEG

DETAIL of LEG

0 1 2 3 4 IN.

CARVING ON CENTER DRAWER

7/8" THICK

DETAIL at B

0 1 2 3
INCHES

0 1 2 3   6   9   12
INCHES

BRASS PULLS

FLUSH

NO CARVING ON REAR LEGS

B

A

FRONT

SIDE

CHAMBER DRESSING TABLE
American 1775 – 1800 (Mahogany)

N O W · I N · T H E · M U S E U M · O F · R H O D E · I S L A N D · S C H O O L · O F · D E S I G N

CHIPPENDALE STYLE CARD TABLE

American Circa 1775

THIS American Chippendale card table is of a later type than that illustrated on Plate 48.

Rectangular in shape, it has a turn-over top, which is supported when unfolded by a pull-out leg. The decoration, in this case, occurs only on the front edge of the upper flap and is gained by a repetition of a restrained gouged motif.

The form of leg most frequently employed by Chippendale was square, usually chamfered on the internal edge, as this example shows. The external edge of the legs is decorated with an ovolo moulding, running down the entire length and giving a lighter and more delicate effect of outline. And a pleasing deviation from ordinary methods is produced by the fluting and partial reeding of the exposed faces of the legs.

The front frieze is of serpentine shape, both in plan and at its lower edge which is moulded and decorated with an incised leaf pattern. The square projecting corners seemingly are supported by small fret-cut brackets, in accordance with the then prevailing Chinese vogue, while the top and aprons at the sides form concave curves.

While this card table shows plainly a Chinese influence in outline, it is classic in decoration.

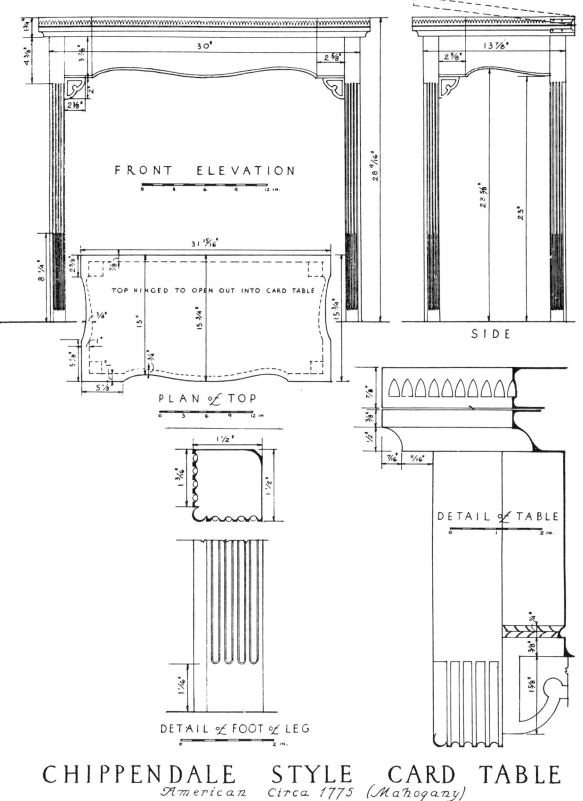

FRONT ELEVATION

PLAN of TOP

SIDE

DETAIL of TABLE

DETAIL of FOOT of LEG

CHIPPENDALE STYLE CARD TABLE
American Circa 1775 (Mahogany)
NOW IN THE BOSTON MUSEUM OF FINE ARTS

LOUIS XV TABLE
French Eighteenth Century

THE style of Louis XV was one of gayety, of luxury, not without charm, and one that was typically French in spirit. The straight lines of the preceding reign had given way to curves and the decoration became daintily florid.

In this charming small table, which is characteristic of the best of the period, not an abrupt angle is to be found. The legs bow outward with an easy grace, the outer and inner lines flowing in long curves into the framework of the table. The elegant pattern carved on the skirt differs on each face. Symmetry of ornamental detail was not in accord with the delicious abandon of these times.

On one face the carved spray of flowers falls naturalistically from a central shell motif over the panelling and the carved scrolls of the skirt. Other motifs, such as the C curve, the flame-like pattern and various kinds of flowers, are placed at will.

The relief of the carving is delicate but varied and energetic. Opposing curves give a balance to the decoration of each face, a daring principle of design, which is admirably applied in this particular piece of furniture.

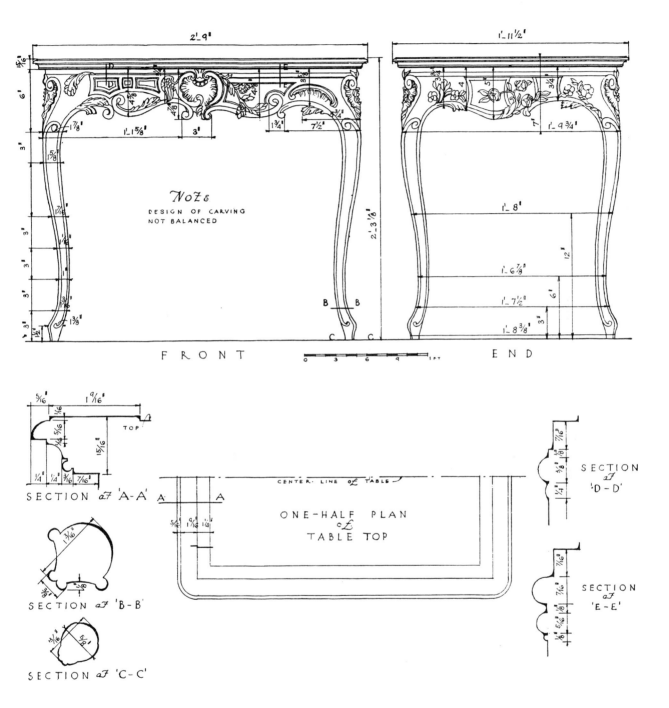

FRONT

END

Note

DESIGN OF CARVING
NOT BALANCED

SECTION of 'A-A'

SECTION of 'B-B'

SECTION of 'C-C'

ONE-HALF PLAN
of
TABLE TOP

CENTER LINE of TABLE

SECTION of 'D-D'

SECTION of 'E-E'

LOUIS XV TABLE
French 18th century (Polished waxed oak)
NOW IN THE METROPOLITAN MUSEUM OF ART

HEPPLEWHITE CARD TABLE

English 1770-1790

THE refined, dignified tables of the style of Hepplewhite show the influence of a cultured people. The carving and inlay with which they were enriched were so delicate in character and workmanship and so admirably designed that these pieces of furniture give the effect of simplicity.

A popular form of small table in the 18th century was the card table, since it was equally useful when closed and placed against the wall as when fulfilling its main function. Great skill on the part of the cabinetmaker is demanded in its execution. The second flap of the example illustrated here forms the top of the table in repose, the moulding underneath, with its bead carved cyma and fillets, forms the top when extended. The serpentine front and sides curve gracefully into square legs, capped with carved leaves in flat relief, and terminate in slender feet, ornamented with leaves and a guilloche pattern. The raised rosettes in the frieze above the front legs are set off with a narrow band of inlay.

The hinged flap lifts so as to form a table top covered with green baize, bordered with a band of mahogany. This is supported by the left hand rear leg which swings on an arm attached to the center of the back.

Panels and borders of very narrow inlay of boxwood enliven the dark mahogany.

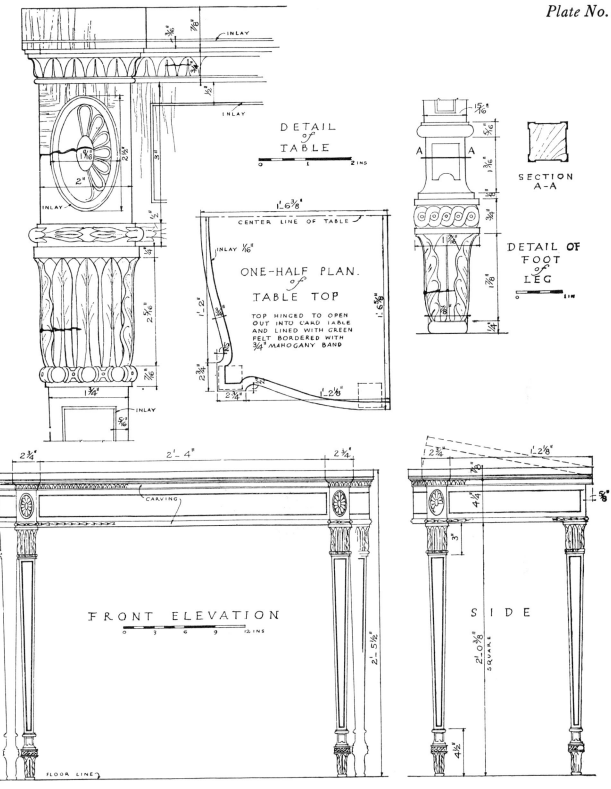

INLAY

¾" ⅞"

¾"

½"

INLAY

2½"

⁹⁄₁₆"

2"

3"

INLAY

½"

¾"

2⅜"

5⁄₁₆"

7⁄₁₆"

1¾"

INLAY

5⁄₁₆"

DETAIL
of
TABLE

0   1   2 INS

CENTER LINE OF TABLE

1'-6⅜"

INLAY 1⁄₁₆"

ONE-HALF PLAN.
of
TABLE TOP

1'-2"

¾"

½"

2¾"

2¾"

1'-2⅛"

1'-6⅝"

TOP HINGED TO OPEN
OUT INTO CARD TABLE
AND LINED WITH GREEN
FELT BORDERED WITH
¾" MAHOGANY BAND

A   A

15⁄₁₆"

5⁄₁₆"

3⁄₁₆"

½"

¾"

1⁷⁄₁₆"

1⅞"

⅞"

¼"

SECTION
A-A

DETAIL **OF**
FOOT
of
LEG

0   1 IN

2¾"   2'-4"   2¾"

CARVING

2'-5½"

FRONT ELEVATION

0   3   6   9   12 INS

2¾"   1'-2⅛"

⅞"

5⁄₈"

4¼"

3"

2'-0⅜"
SQUARE

4½"

SIDE

FLOOR LINE

HEPPLEWHITE CARD TABLE
English 1770-90 (Mahogany)
N O W · I N · T H E · M E T R O P O L I T A N · M U S E U M · O F · A R T

HEPPLEWHITE SIDE TABLE

English 1780-1790

THIS handsomely decorated satinwood table is one of a pair, each half serving as a console table when used separately, or, when used together, the whole forming an oval topped table.

The use of inlay, which was one of the most striking features of the later years of the Hepplewhite influence, has been here treated in an exceedingly skilful and adroit manner. The table top, like many examples of this period, is beautifully inlaid in colored woods of sycamore, commonly known as harewood, satinwood, rosewood, holly and tulipwood. The inlaid medallions spaced at intervals around the table top and the flower motifs at each leg are etched in black, whereas the half-oval fan at the center of the top is both etched and painted.

The usual carved flutes on the square, tapered legs of Hepplewhite furniture are here represented by flutes of inlay, the panels of the apron being similarly treated. The legs are edged with narrow bands of ebony. A high French polish tends to accentuate the subtle coloring of the inlaid designs.

Simplicity of line and grace of ornament make this table one of the most elegant of its kind.

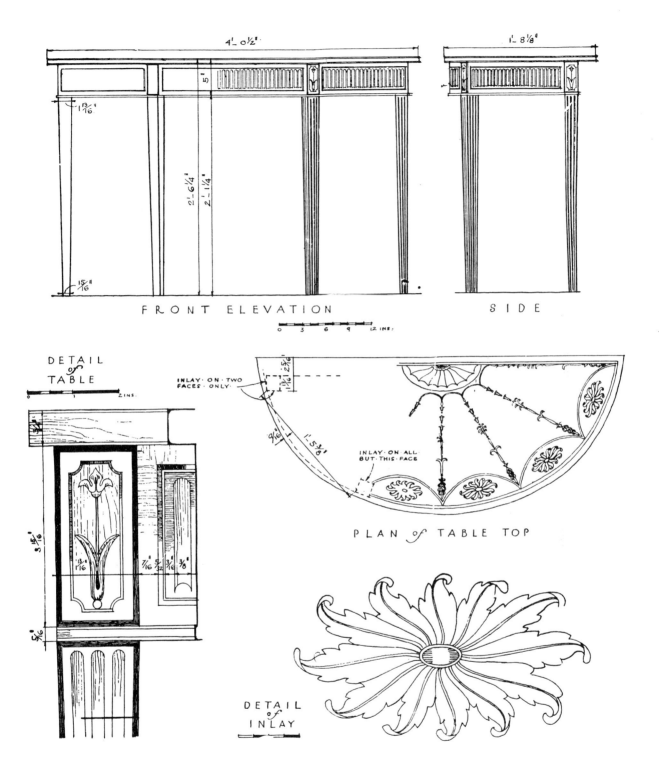

FRONT ELEVATION

SIDE

DETAIL
of
TABLE

INLAY ON TWO
FACES ONLY

INLAY ON ALL
BUT THIS FACE

PLAN of TABLE TOP

DETAIL
of
INLAY

HEPPLEWHITE SIDE TABLE
English 1780-90 (Satinwood)
NOW IN THE METROPOLITAN MUSEUM OF ART

HEPPLEWHITE DRESSING TABLE
American 1790-1800

AMONG the numerous types of tables designed by Hepplewhite and copied by his contemporaries was the dressing table, an excellent example of which is illustrated here. This table, of mahogany, made by American artisans, remains to tell us of the keen judgment and discernment of the designers of that period. The front is swelled, the legs slender and the otherwise severe simplicity of contour is relieved by the introduction of a semi-ellipse at the lower line of the frame and by carved brackets of charming design. The drawers are ornamented with satinwood panels of interesting grain and bordered with minutely and intricately inlaid bands of ebony and holly.

Strings of tapered husks top the front legs, and near the foot the inlay takes the form of the Greek fret—a classic pattern used extensively by Hepplewhite.

Of the four drawers only the smaller, center one is fitted with compartments, and this one with three compartments at each side, leaving an open space through the center.

The brass drawer pulls are handsomely ornamented, adding a final note of richness to this graciously adorned but unpretentious piece of furniture.

In accordance with the custom of the time a high French polish was applied to this table.

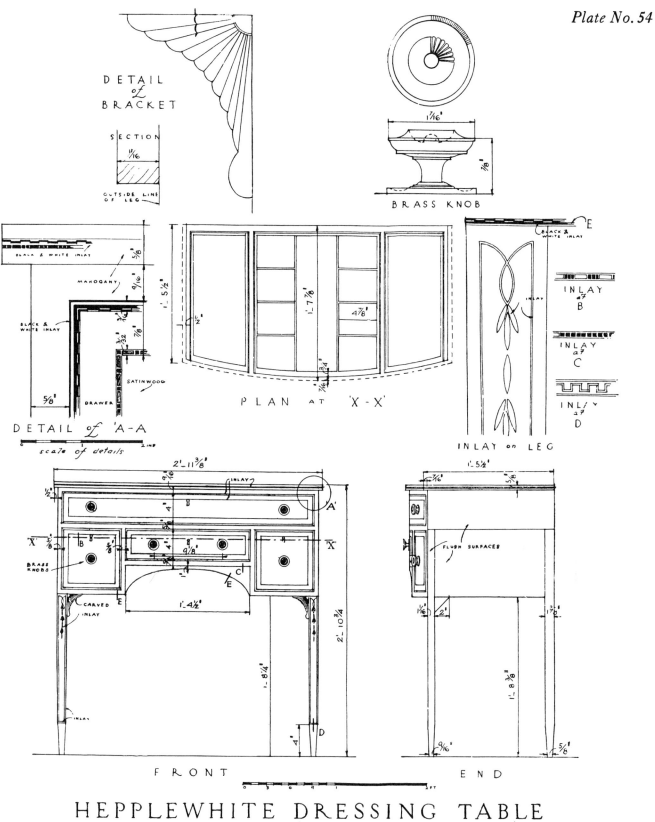

DETAIL of BRACKET

SECTION

OUTSIDE LINE OF LEG

BRASS KNOB

BLACK & WHITE INLAY

MAHOGANY

BLACK & WHITE INLAY

SATINWOOD

DRAWER

DETAIL of 'A-A

scale of details

PLAN at 'X-X'

BLACK & WHITE INLAY

INLAY

INLAY at B

INLAY at C

INLAY at D

INLAY on LEG

FRONT

BRASS KNOBS

CARVED INLAY

INLAY

END

FLUSH SURFACES

HEPPLEWHITE DRESSING TABLE
American 1790-1800 (Mahogany and Satinwood)
NOW IN THE METROPOLITAN MUSEUM OF ART

"BEAU-BRUMMEL" DRESSING TABLE
American Late XVIII Century

A TYPE of dressing table popular in England throughout the 18th century was one with a boxed top composed of two flaps, hinged at the outer edges of the framework. When opened, a central mirror, together with compartments for the holding of toilet accessories, is exposed. The main carcase work of the table is fitted with drawers.

Of this type and period is the so-called "Beau-Brummel" dressing table shown on these two pages. It was probably executed in New York. Fashioned with satinwood, it is of unadorned simplicity with the exception of the relieving borders at the drawers. These borders are of bands of the same wood and are edged with inlaid stringings of a black wood—presumably ebony. This dark inlay

is also used to accentuate the tapering edges of the legs. An offsetting band of ebony, conforming to the curve of the knee-opening at the center, is carried along the lower edge of the body framework.

A pull-up mirror on ratchets, flanked by two compartments of differing equipment, fills the space, indicated by the false upper drawer. The lids of the four symmetrical subdivisions of these compartments are of mahogany, as is, likewise, the frame of the mirror. Ivory moulded knobs are supplied for the mirror and compartment lids, whereas wooden knobs, also moulded, are provided for the drawer pulls.

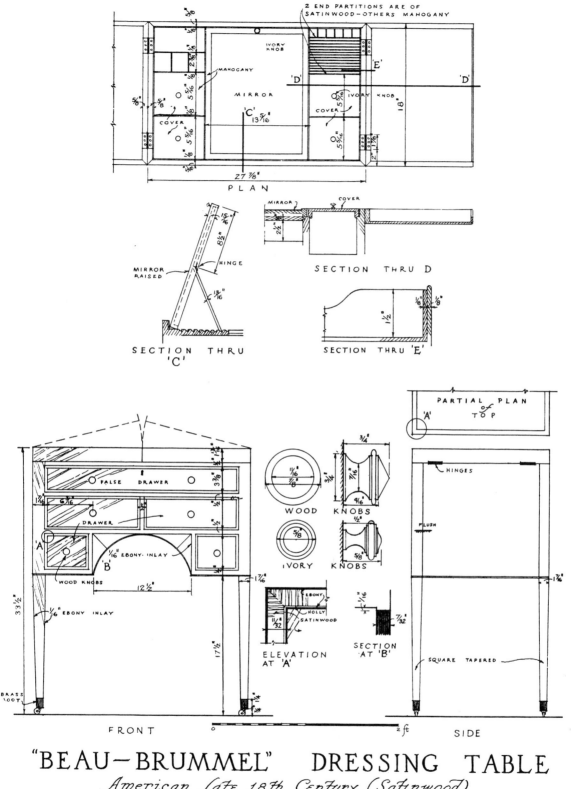

"BEAU–BRUMMEL" DRESSING TABLE
American Late 18th Century (Satinwood)
OWNED BY MR & MRS LOUIS G MYERS

PEMBROKE TABLE
American 1775-1800

AMONG the variations of the Hepplewhite and Sheraton styles was the "Pembroke" table, so-called in honor of Lady Pembroke from whom the first commission came. This name is applied to a type of table with drop leaves which are supported, when extended, by two brackets which swing under the top. When closed these brackets fold in pockets against the table and allow the drop leaves to fall in a vertical position.

The charming Pembroke table illustrated is of curly sycamore veneer on mahogany. The legs are straight and tapering, edged with lines of holly and ornamented at the top with inlaid medallions of etched leaves. The top is cut in serpentine curves around which runs a band of tulipwood. Three large oval designs of inlaid leaves in conventionalized pattern, set off with brush work and etching, decorate the top and drop leaves. Although both ends are provided with turned wooden drawer pulls, there is but one drawer and that running the entire depth. The drawer faces are slightly curved and veneered with a panel of sycamore.

Since these tables were usually designed for breakfast tables they were consequently small.

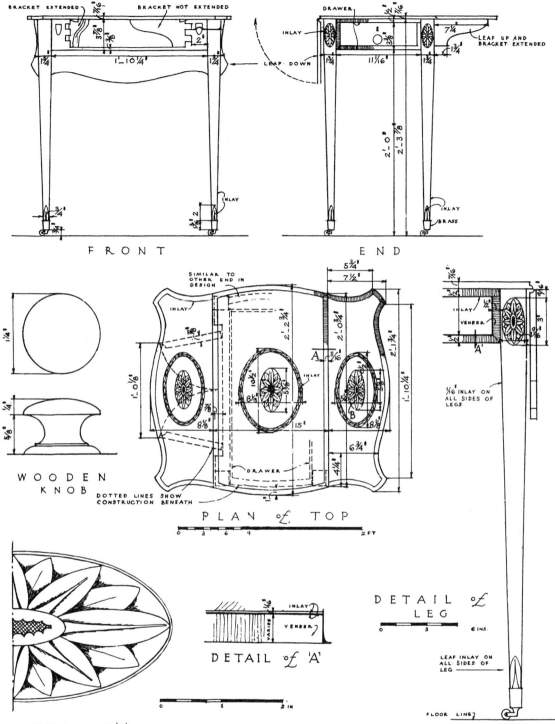

FRONT

END

WOODEN KNOB

DETAIL of 'B'

PLAN of TOP

DOTTED LINES SHOW CONSTRUCTION BENEATH

DETAIL of 'A'

DETAIL of LEG

PEMBROKE TABLE STYLE of HEPPLEWHITE
American about 1775-1800 (Sycamore on Mahogany)
NOW IN THE METROPOLITAN MUSEUM OF ART

PEMBROKE TABLE
American 1790-1800

THE most popular types of the "Pembroke" or hinged-flap table, which was essentially a pattern of the Sheraton period, were those with oval and square tops, either plain or shaped. This example, contemporaneous with the table preceding, is of the oval-topped type. At the height of its fashion, the Pembroke table was considered the most useful of its class and generally combined handsome decoration with excellent craftsmanship.

With the exception of the oval shaped top, this small piece of furniture differs little in general form and construction from the foregoing example. It is less ornate in its applied ornamentation. A wide band of mahogany veneer is used to border the panel of the drawer, the latter being edged with a beading of like wood. Small inlaid bands of contrasting wood outline the edge of the oval top and run down the corners of the legs. Tapered chains of the husk pattern are inlaid at the top of each outer face of the legs, while the motif, directly above these pendants, is of satinwood and shaded by means of painting. Brass feet conforming to the unbroken taper terminate the legs.

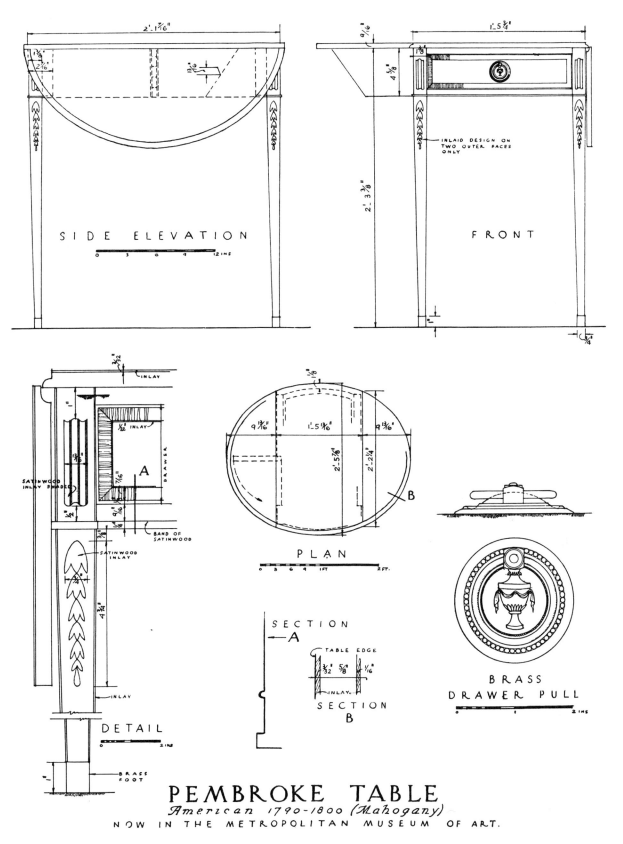

SIDE ELEVATION

FRONT

INLAID DESIGN ON
TWO OUTER FACES
ONLY

PLAN

DETAIL

SECTION
A

TABLE EDGE

SECTION
B

BRASS
DRAWER PULL

SATINWOOD
INLAY SHADED

INLAY

DRAWER

BAND OF
SATINWOOD

SATINWOOD
INLAY

INLAY

BRASS
FOOT

INLAY

PEMBROKE TABLE
American 1790-1800 (Mahogany)
NOW IN THE METROPOLITAN MUSEUM OF ART.

FOLDING TABLE, STYLE OF
SHERATON

SHERATON, a master of straight lines, used in his construction the rectangular, high perpendicular outlines of slender structural form. He also excelled in the use of the tapered leg and in the adaptation of the serpentine swell.

An unusually fine example of an American table, evolved upon the lines of the Sheraton period, is that of the folding type shown here. The legs, typical of this era, are based upon Louis XVI models. They are round and tapering, with the shaped shaft finely reeded and terminating in a delicately tapered foot.

The apron follows the serpentine curve of the table top and is rounded at the corners to conform to the outline of the supporting legs.

Inlay and veneered panels, rather than carving, follows the Sheraton usage. A handsome decorative effect is here obtained by the use of satinwood and ebony inlay forming oval and rectangular panels, and also by the introduction of small bands of inlay composed of holly and ebony.

The woods most generally used at this time were mahogany and satinwood, the latter being employed to a greater extent by Sheraton than by his contemporaries.

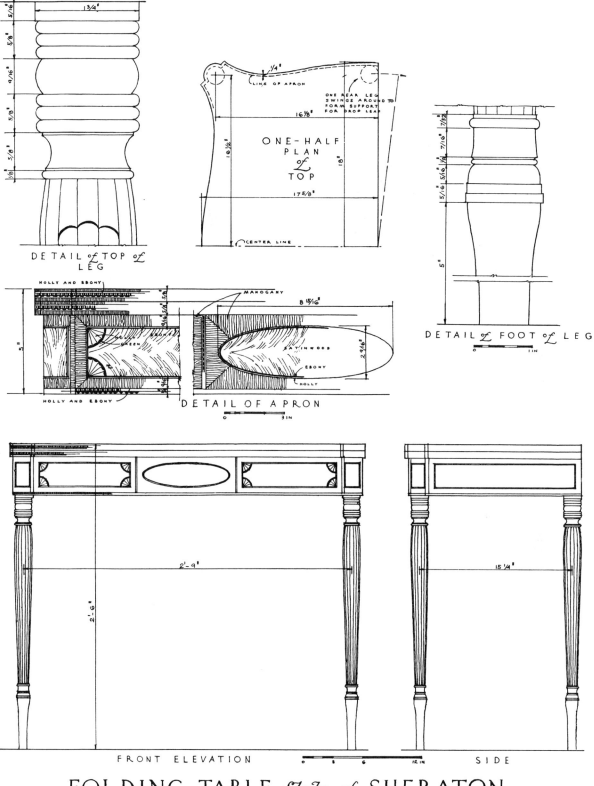

13/4"

5/16"
5/8"
9/16"
5/8"
5/8"

DETAIL of TOP of
LEG

1/4"
LINE OF APRON

ONE REAR LEG
SWINGS AROUND TO
FORM SUPPORT
FOR DROP LEAF

16 1/8"

ONE-HALF
PLAN
of
TOP

16 1/2"

18"

17 5/8"

CENTER LINE

7/32"
7/16"
1/4"
5/16"
5/16"

5"

DETAIL of FOOT of LEG

0   1 IN

HOLLY AND EBONY
5/8"
9/16"
MAHOGANY

5"

HOLLY
EBONY
GREEN

8 15/16"
SATINWOOD
EBONY
HOLLY

9/16"
HOLLY AND EBONY

DETAIL OF APRON

0   3 IN

2 9/16"

2'-9"

2'-6"

15 1/4"

FRONT ELEVATION

0   6   12 IN

SIDE

FOLDING TABLE *Style of* SHERATON
American 1790-1800 (Mahogany and satinwood)
NOW IN THE METROPOLITAN MUSEUM OF ART

SHERATON BREAKFAST TABLE
American 1775-1800

A VARIETY of small breakfast tables, designed so as to harmonize with the style of furniture then prevailing for bedrooms, were made in the 18th century. The custom of eating breakfast in the bedroom, however, seems to date from a much earlier period.

This example, executed in mahogany and modeled on Sheraton lines, is of rectangular construction and is provided with flaps supported upon hinged wooden brackets or wings of the Pembroke principle.

The combination of the straight line with the curve, favored in the designs of Sheraton, is represented in this piece of furniture. Serpentine curves outline the drop leaves and shape the front faces of the drawer ends, which, with their fluting, carry out the decorative effect of the legs. This gives to the top, when extended, a pleasing contour which is skilfully emphasized by the inlaid border of satinwood running about the edge of the top.

The four legs are square and tapered. Their perpendicular aspect is heightened by fluted and reeded surfaces.

Oval paterae, composed of inlay of satinwood, accent the top of each leg and give additional evidence of the carefully placed ornamentation exercised by the craftsmen of this school.

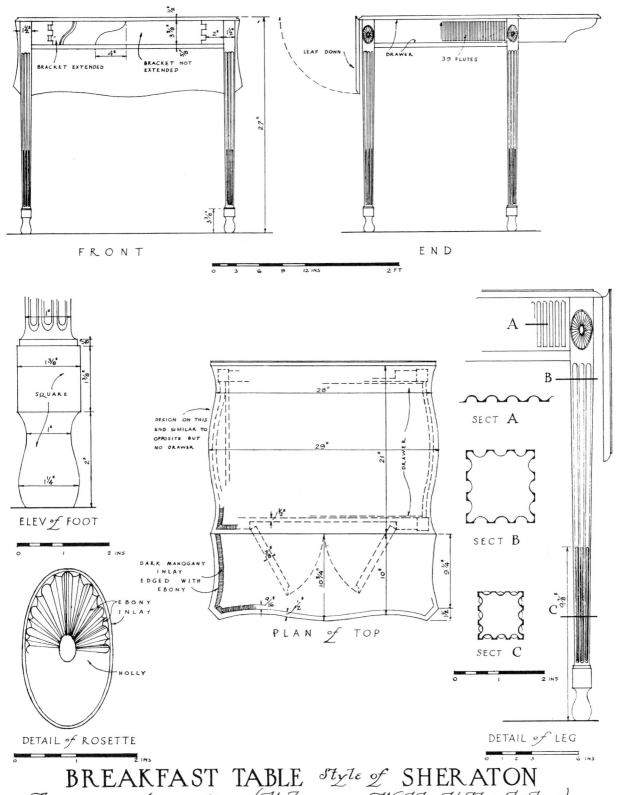

FRONT

END

0 3 6 9 12 INS   2 FT

1½"

3⅜"
⅝"
BRACKET EXTENDED
BRACKET NOT
EXTENDED
4"
2" 1½"

27"

3⅜"

LEAF DOWN
DRAWER
39 FLUTES

ELEV *of* FOOT

1"
⅝"
1⅜"
1⅜"
SQUARE
1"
1¼"
2"

0 1 2 INS

DETAIL *of* ROSETTE

EBONY
INLAY
HOLLY

0 1 2 INS

DESIGN ON THIS
END SIMILAR TO
OPPOSITE BUT
NO DRAWER

28"
29"
21"
DRAWER
1½"
10¾"
10"
9¼"
1½"

DARK MAHOGANY
INLAY
EDGED WITH
EBONY

PLAN *of* TOP

A
B
SECT A
SECT B
C
SECT C

0 1 2 INS

DETAIL *of* LEG

9⅜"

0 1 2 3   6 INS

BREAKFAST TABLE *Style of* SHERATON
American   1775 – 1800 (Mahogany With Holly Inlay)
N O W · I N · T H E · M U S E U M · O F · R H O D E · I S L A N D · S C H O O L · O F · D E S I G N .

ONE OF A NEST OF TABLES

English Style of the Adam Brothers Late 1800

AN exemplification of the sober mahogany style sponsored by the brothers Adam in England is this principal unit of a "nest of tables." Economy of space prompted the manufacture of these "quartetto tables," as they were originally called. The complete set consisted of four small tables, similar in design and construction and graduated in size so that when not in use they fit snugly one below the other. In this example each top of the three smaller tables slides into a rebate cut into the top supporting member at the side. When separated they were intended for writing, or, as one of the original designers of these tables stated, "to prevent company rising from their seats when taking refreshments."

The light and graceful treatment of the rectangular proportions found in this example is characteristic of Adam design. Likewise characteristic is the classic inspiration embodied in the column-like form of the delicately tapered legs.

A method of decoration much favored by the brothers Adam is the representation of decorative motifs by inlaid woods. In the table, under discussion, the flutings on the legs, the paneling at top and the inlaid stringing at the feet are in accordance with this preference.

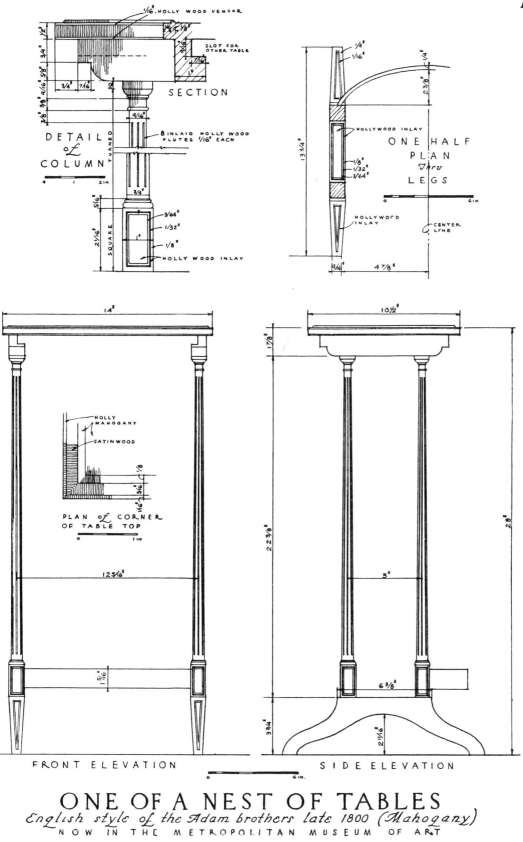

1/16" HOLLY WOOD VENEER

SECTION

SLOT FOR OTHER TABLE

DETAIL
of
COLUMN

8 INLAID HOLLY WOOD FLUTES 1/16" EACH

0   1   2 IN.

TURNED

SQUARE

3/64"
1/32"
1/8"

HOLLY WOOD INLAY

ONE HALF
PLAN
Thru
LEGS

HOLLYWOOD INLAY

HOLLYWOOD INLAY

CENTER LINE

0   6 IN.

HOLLY
MAHOGANY

SATINWOOD

PLAN of CORNER
OF TABLE TOP

0   1 IN.

FRONT ELEVATION

SIDE ELEVATION

0   6 IN.

ONE OF A NEST OF TABLES
English style of the Adam brothers late 1800 (Mahogany)
N O W   I N   T H E   M E T R O P O L I T A N   M U S E U M   O F   A R T

DUNCAN PHYFE DROP LEAF TABLE

American 1800-1810

TO DUNCAN PHYFE, the New York cabinet maker, is credited some of the most beautiful furniture of American craftsmanship. At first his work shows inspiration from both Hepplewhite and Sheraton, but this was combined, in the early years of the 19th century, with certain features of Directoire and Empire origin.

The illustrated example is of that period of his work which embodies elements of the Sheraton style. This mahogany drop-leaf table is supported at the ends by coupled colonnettes, resting upon concave legs, sweeping outward and terminating in brass lion's feet. The legs are in the characteristic form with acanthus leaves and reeding

carved on the surfaces. The same decorative treatment is applied to the colonnettes. Delicate grooving ornaments the edge of the table and also the drop leaves, which are supported, when extended, by two shaped brackets. A narrow beading finishes the drawers. The long stretchers connecting the legs are formed by double spindles of excellent turning and ornamented with a band of reeding at the center.

An unobtrusive band of mahogany inlay follows the outer line of the table top and is repeated on the drawer faces and on the vertical block immediately under the coupled colonnettes.

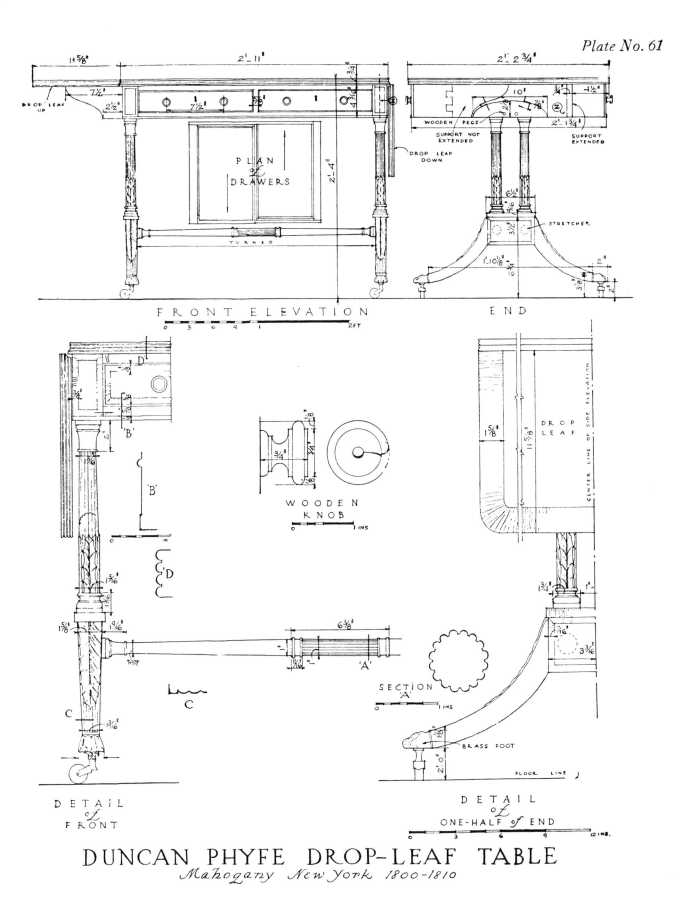

FRONT ELEVATION

END

PLAN of DRAWERS

TURNED

WOODEN KNOB

SECTION 'A'

DETAIL of FRONT

DETAIL of ONE-HALF of END

DUNCAN PHYFE DROP-LEAF TABLE
Mahogany New York 1800-1810

DUNCAN PHYFE DINING TABLE

American Early XIX Century

SEVERAL types of tables were designed by Duncan Phyfe. They vary chiefly in the form of leg structure used. Some were supported upon straight reeded legs which were placed at the corners of the table top, while others were supported upon pedestals. The pedestal took various forms such as the crossed lyres, or colonnettes resting upon a platform which was in turn supported upon concave legs flaring outward. An example of the latter type is shown on the preceding plate.

The third group and that of the dining room table shown on these pages consists of the solid turned pedestal combined with outward-curving legs. These legs were either three or four in number. In this particular example the edge of the table top proper is relieved by horizontal beading and this manner of decoration, so much favored by Duncan Phyfe, is also applied to the vase shape of the pedestal, and to the lower part of the curved legs, while the characteristic acanthus leaf ornaments the top portion of the legs.

The two turned intermediate legs fold and rest under the table top when not in use, that is to say when the table is not extended.

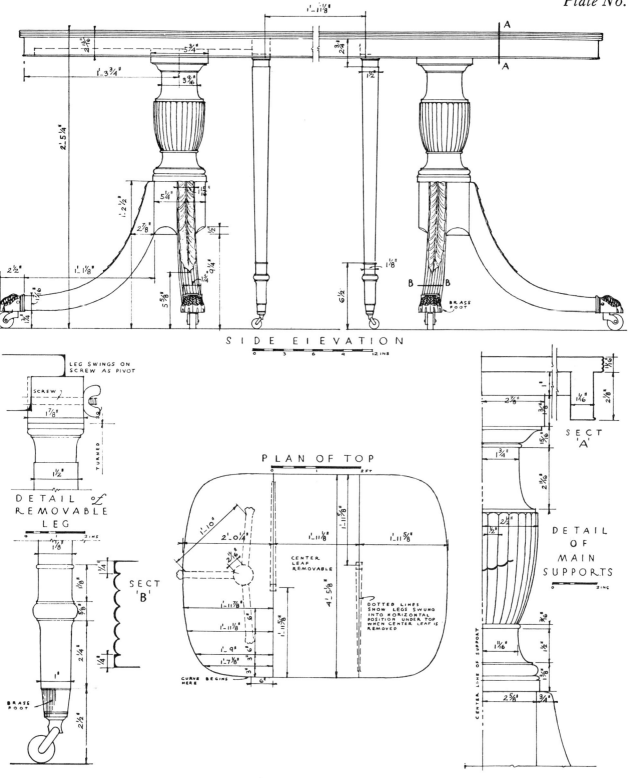

SIDE ELEVATION

0 3 6 4   12 INS

LEG SWINGS ON
SCREW AS PIVOT

SCREW

DETAIL of
REMOVABLE
LEG

SECT
'B'

BRASS
FOOT

PLAN OF TOP

CENTER
LEAF
REMOVABLE

DOTTED LINES
SHOW LEGS SWUNG
INTO HORIZONTAL
POSITION UNDER TOP
WHEN CENTER LEAF IS
REMOVED

CURVE BEGINS
HERE

SECT
'A'

DETAIL
OF
MAIN
SUPPORTS

CENTER LINE OF SUPPORT

BRASS
FOOT

DUNCAN PHYFE DINING TABLE
American Early 19th century (Mahogany)
NOW IN THE METROPOLITAN MUSEUM OF ART

JACOBEAN SIDEBOARD
English 1660-1688

THIS Jacobean sideboard exemplifies, in its proportions and in its well placed decorative details, the simplicity in which some of the furniture at this time was executed, and which contrasts sharply with those contemporaneous pieces which, in outline and by the introduction of superfluous detail, appear confused in their elements of design.

The general adoption of drawers was an outgrowth of this period and were here introduced in the rectilinear framework which is supported upon three front legs and two at the back. Four drawers fill the carcase; two smaller ones at the center, which are flanked by larger ones, each of which is subdivided into two panels. The base of these drawers is ornamented with mouldings of geometric formation, characteristic of the 17th century. Large oval brass knobs are placed at the center of each of these panels.

The three front leg supports are of light proportions and are garnished with cylindrical turnings. These legs, together with those at the rear, are linked together, below the drawer framework, with an apron of a bold cut-out pattern. The intermediate front leg forms the axis for the symmetrical treatment of both drawer arrangement and the cut-out design of the connecting apron.

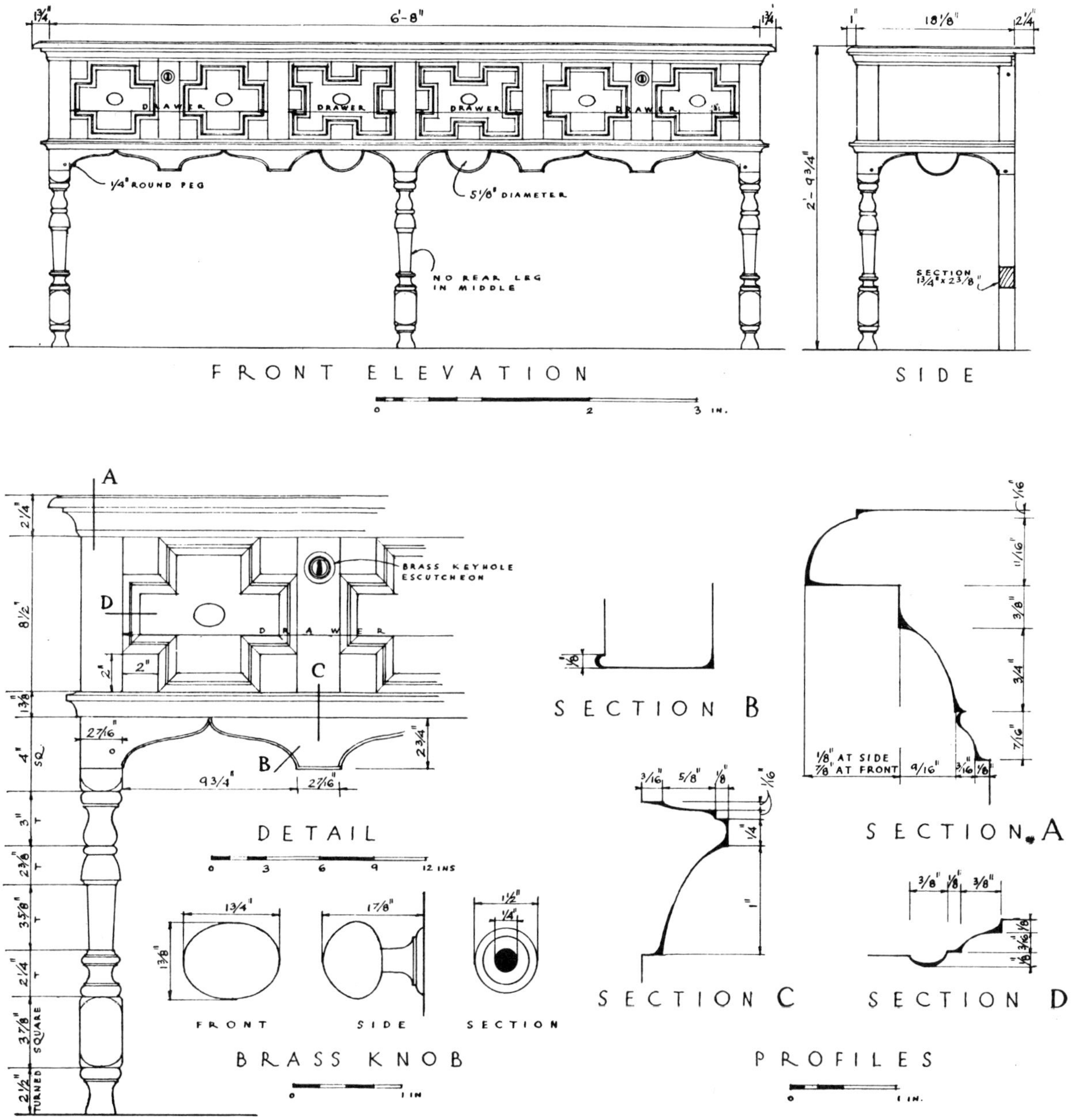
1¾"
6'-8"
1¾"
DRAWER
DRAWER
DRAWER
DRAWER
¼" ROUND PEG
5⅛" DIAMETER
NO REAR LEG IN MIDDLE
FRONT ELEVATION
0
2
3 IN.
1"
18⅛"
2¼"
2'-9¾"
SECTION 1¾" x 2⅜"
SIDE
A
2¼"
8½"
BRASS KEYHOLE ESCUTCHEON
D
DRAWER
2"
2"
C
1⅜"
2 7/16"
4" SQ
B
9¾"
2 7/16"
2¾"
3" T
2⅜" T
3⅝" T
2¼" T
3⅞" SQUARE
2½" TURNED
DETAIL
0
3
6
9
12 INS
1¾"
1⅜"
1⅞"
1½"
¼"
FRONT
SIDE
SECTION
BRASS KNOB
0
1 IN
⅛"
SECTION B
3/16"
⅝"
⅛"
1/16"
¼"
1"
SECTION C
1/16
11/16"
⅜"
¾"
7/16"
⅛" AT SIDE
⅞" AT FRONT
9/16"
3/16"
⅛"
SECTION A
⅜"
⅛"
⅜"
⅛"
3/16"
⅛"
SECTION D
PROFILES
0
1 IN.

JACOBEAN SIDE BOARD

English 1660–1688 (Oak)

SIDEBOARD, STYLE OF HEPPLEWHITE

American Last Quarter XVIII Century

IT IS generally considered that the point of difference between the sideboards, sponsored by Hepplewhite and those in the Sheraton manner, lay in the contour of the carcase; those of Hepplewhite being generally of serpentine or straight front; whereas, Sheraton usually preferred a bowed front swelling out from rectangular corners. There are, however, exceptions to this belief, as is illustrated by the sideboard executed along Sheraton models and shown on the following plate.

The serpentine front was undoubtedly a favorite incorporation of Hepplewhite's, either by its adoption for the entire front or by confining it to the central portion with flanking straight or convex wings. The central portion of this example is equipped with a large drawer above a compartment, closed behind two swinging drawers provided with lock and key, and at the ends by cellerette drawers. These cellerette drawers were frequently provided with several divisions and lined with lead to hold wine bottles.

It was the aim of Hepplewhite to "unite elegancy and utility and blend the useful with the agreeable." Many of the salient features of the Hepplewhite school, which in England covered the period of 1780 to 1800, are fused into the furniture of American origin of that date.

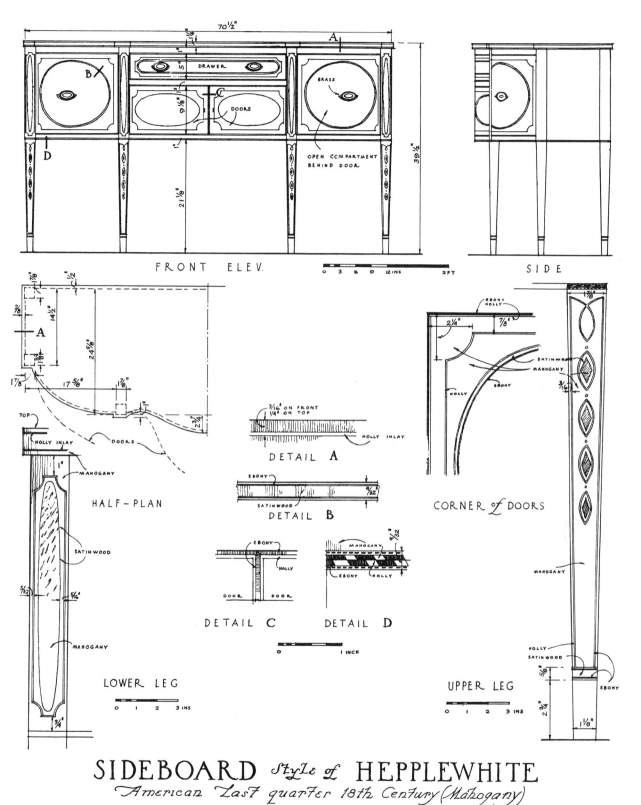

FRONT ELEV.

SIDE

HALF-PLAN

DETAIL A

DETAIL B

DETAIL C   DETAIL D

CORNER of DOORS

LOWER LEG

UPPER LEG

SIDEBOARD *Style of* HEPPLEWHITE
American Last quarter 18th Century (Mahogany)
NOW IN THE MUSEUM OF RHODE ISLAND SCHOOL OF DESIGN

SMALL SIDEBOARD

American 1775-1800

IN ENGLAND, about the middle of the 18th century, the appointments of the dining room began to receive especial attention. At that time they commenced to make sideboards and side tables for use solely in this room. This supplanted the use in the dining room of tables which were equally serviceable in the reception room, drawing room or hall, as had been the custom in the generations preceding. Small sideboards, such as the one shown opposite, were intended originally as serving tables, to be used as adjuncts to sideboards.

Drawers and cupboards were introduced into the framework of side boards which stood upon four or six legs. Under the guidance of such designers as Shearer, Sheraton and Hepplewhite, a most

graceful and useful piece of furniture was evolved.

This small sideboard, executed in America, follows the straight fronted type much favored by Hepplewhite, and is delightful in its pleasing proportions and in the delicacy of its construction. The use of brass fittings, of spread eagle design, on the flanking double drawers becomes most effective by its introduction of a markedly contrasting element. The restrained use of holly stringing on the mahogany framework, offset so skilfully by panels of dark mottled mahogany, is particularly admirable. The broadened space, obtained by the downward flare of the lower rail of the case, is adequately filled by a modest spray of hollywood inlay.

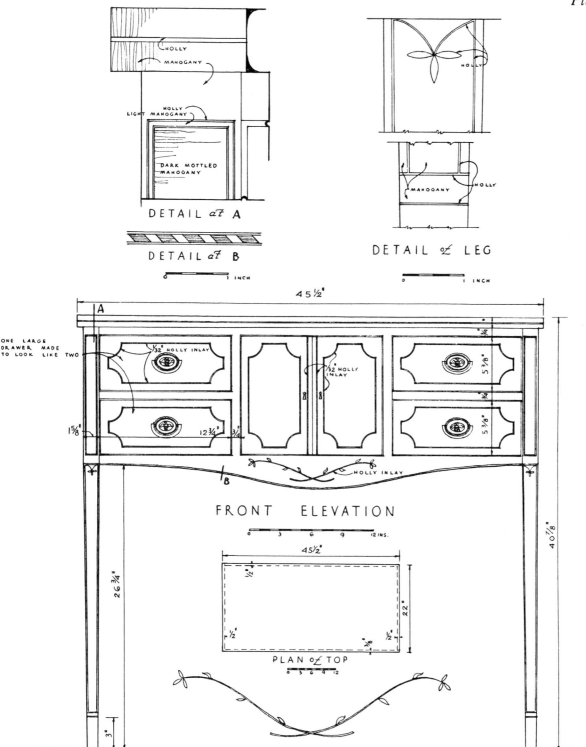

DETAIL *at* A

DETAIL *at* B

0   1 INCH

DETAIL *of* LEG

0   1 INCH

HOLLY

MAHOGANY

HOLLY
LIGHT MAHOGANY

DARK MOTTLED
MAHOGANY

HOLLY

MAHOGANY   HOLLY

45½"

A

ONE LARGE
DRAWER MADE
TO LOOK LIKE TWO

¹/₃₂" HOLLY INLAY

¹/₃₂" HOLLY
INLAY

¾"

5 ³/₈"

¾"

5 ³/₈"

1 ⁵/₈"   12 ¾"   ¾"

HOLLY INLAY

B

FRONT ELEVATION

0   3   6   9   12 INS.

26 ¾"

40 ⁷/₈"

45½"

½"

½"   ³/₈"   ½"

22"

3"

PLAN *of* TOP

0   3 6   9   12

SMALL SIDE BOARD *Style of* HEPPLEWHITE
American 1775-1800 (Mahogany with Holly Inlay)
NOW IN THE PENDLETON COLLECTION - RHODE ISLAND SCHOOL OF DESIGN PROVIDENCE R.I.

SIDEBOARD, STYLE OF SHERATON

American 1790-1800

THIS American made sideboard, based on the Sheraton vogue, is of unusual interest in that it incorporates the serpentine curve—so much favored by Sheraton's contemporary, Hepplewhite—in the central portion and between the convex flanking sides. The contour of the countershelf between the two intermediate legs does not, however, conform to the serpentine outline below, but instead is of circular shape.

Six tapering legs support the superstructure and are extended through the body to the underside of the top. The rear legs and those corresponding at the front show flat faces while the two intermediate supports are five sided and are set at an angle with two decorated faces exposed.

The rectangular lines of the paneled inlay accentuate the structure of the body. Handsome bands of mahogany veneering edged with stringing of holly, combined with mahogany, border the drawer panels. Four motifs of fan design carried out in shaded inlay of satinwood accent the corners of each of the convex cellerette drawers, as well as, those of the two central hinged doors of serpentine shape. At the top of each front leg face and immediately below the countershelf is a design of contrasting inlaid strips simulating a reeded motif.

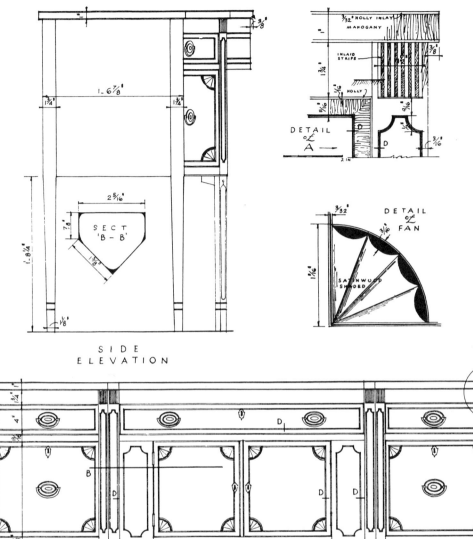

S I D E
E L E V A T I O N

DETAIL
of
A

DETAIL of
FAN

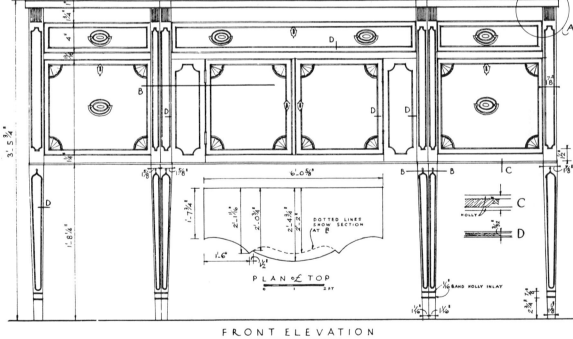

F R O N T   E L E V A T I O N

PLAN of TOP

DOTTED LINES
SHOW SECTION
AT B

SIDE BOARD *Style of* SHERATON
American 1790-1800 (Mahogany)
N O W   I N   T H E   M E T R O P O L I T A N   M U S E U M   O F   A R T

MIXING TABLE

American About 1800

FOLLOWING Sheraton precedent, this mixing table is an unusually fine example of American workmanship during the early years of the new Republic. It has been attributed to a Baltimore craftsman. During that flourishing period in Maryland, patronage was liberally extended to a variety of skilled artisans, particularly silversmiths and cabinet makers.

The large drawers at either end, presumably for the holding of bottles, are separated by a table top, in which is inset a piece of white marble. This particular material was used in this place in order to obviate the possibility of the mahogany being injured when beverages were mixed. A tambour top rolls down and closes over this mixing space.

This table is distinctive in its exquisite execution and in its delicate design. The legs are of the slender tapering type and inlaid with paneled borders of satinwood of varying outline. The same wood is inlaid, in combination with other woods on the apron of the table, in most interesting designs, composed of rectangular panels terminating in leaf motifs and in egg-shaped panels. Large oval inlays decorate both the exterior and interior sides of the bottle drawers.

The wood used is a beautiful grained mahogany. In place of the customary brasses, turned knobs of mahogany are used to operate the end compartments.

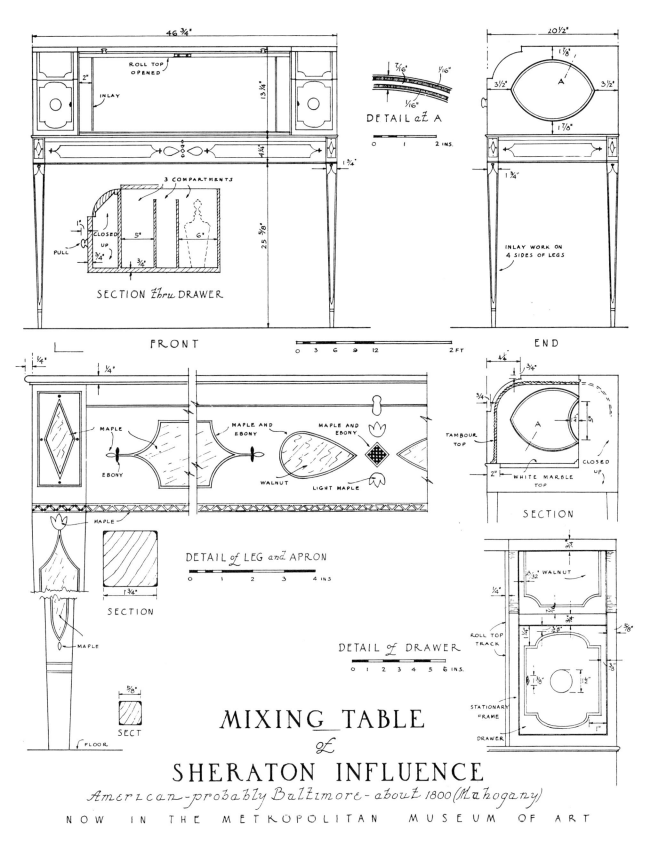

46 ¾"

ROLL TOP
OPENED

2"

INLAY

13 ¼"

4 ¼"

1 ¾"

3 COMPARTMENTS

1"

CLOSED
UP

PULL

¾"

5"

¾"

6"

25 ⅝"

SECTION *thru* DRAWER

FRONT

⅞6"

¼6"

DETAIL *at* A

¼6"

0   1   2 INS.

20 ½"

1 ⅞"

3 ½"   A   3 ½"

1 ⅞"

1 ¾"

INLAY WORK ON
4 SIDES OF LEGS

END

0 3 6 9 12   2 FT

¼"

¼"

MAPLE

EBONY

MAPLE AND
EBONY

WALNUT

MAPLE AND
EBONY

LIGHT MAPLE

MAPLE

MAPLE

SECTION

1 ¾"

DETAIL *of* LEG *and* APRON

0   1   2   3   4 INS.

⅝"

SECT

FLOOR

¼"

¾"

¾"

TAMBOUR
TOP

A

4"

5"

CLOSED
UP

2"   WHITE MARBLE
TOP

SECTION

¾"

3/32" WALNUT

¼"

¾"

ROLL TOP
TRACK

3/8"

⅝"

1 ¼"

3/8"

1 ½"

1 3/8"

STATIONARY
FRAME

DRAWER

1"

⅜"

DETAIL *of* DRAWER

0 1 2 3 4 5 6 INS.

MIXING TABLE
of
SHERATON INFLUENCE

American—probably Baltimore—about 1800 (Mahogany)

N O W   I N   T H E   M E T R O P O L I T A N   M U S E U M   O F   A R T

ITALIAN CHEST
Florentine XV Century

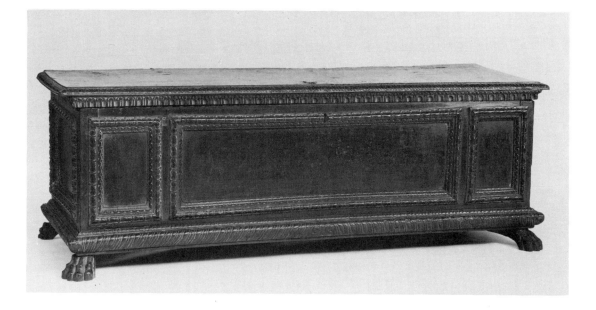

THIS Italian chest, imposing both in size and in its stately treatment, serves two purposes, that of a chest and also a seat. It is characteristic of the stylistic trend of furniture of the Renaissance, when an architectural character was infused into all the decorative arts, including that of furniture making.

The severe, rectilinear lines of the structure are relieved by the use of bold richly moulded members. This robust chest rests upon massive feet, carved in the form of lion's paws. The top of the chest, which is hinged at the back, lifts up to form a lid. The edges of this lid, as well as the mouldings directly beneath, are richly carved in motifs derived from classic sources. Panels enrich the sides and front of the chest body. They are sunken and surrounded with a moulding of bolection type, which is also handsomely carved in the same spirit as the mouldings of the lid. At the base the chest is finished with a massive thumb moulding, again richly ornamented.

It will be noticed that, in this example, the decoration is entirely confined to the various mouldings, and with the exception of the fillets no member of these shaped surfaces remains unadorned by carving.

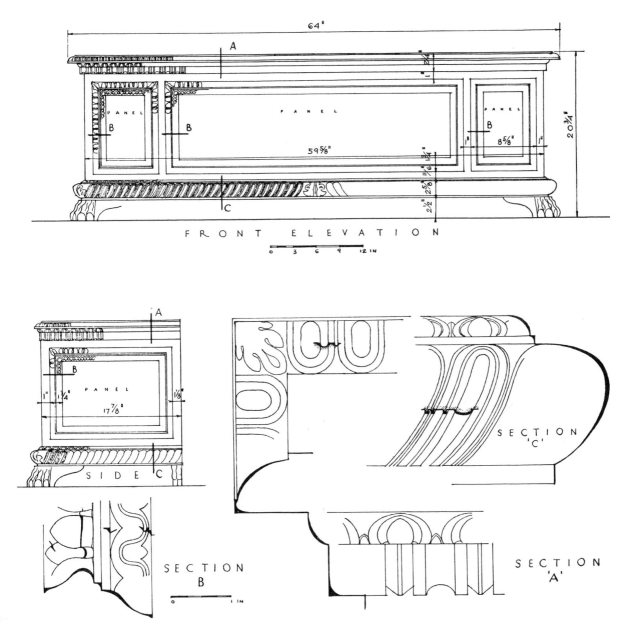

FRONT ELEVATION

64"

20¾"

PANEL

PANEL 59⅝"

PANEL 8⅝"

SIDE

PANEL 17⅞"

SECTION 'C'

SECTION B

SECTION 'A'

ITALIAN CHEST
Florentine XV Century (Walnut)
NOW IN THE METROPOLITAN MUSEUM OF ART

CUPBOARD

English XV Century

ENGLISH furniture of any description during the 15th century was limited both in variety and amount. Numerous chests, however, were made at that time as well as in the preceding century. The furniture makers were then less skillful and resourceful than the carpenters, and the latter occupied a position of greater importance.

In construction these chests were of a primitive type, being made from solid boards held in place by wrought iron nails or wooden pegs. The standing cupboard, such as the example illustrated on these two pages, was an important piece of furniture during the 15th century. The arrangement of the central door (double doors not appearing until the close of the 17th century) fashioned as it is from one piece of wood and flanked by two upright boards extending below the carcase to act as feet, is typical of the design and craftsmanship of this period. The sides are prolonged to the floor, the front being cut and shaped to form a generous opening.

The door as well as the broad flanking uprights are ornamented with pierced bold carving in crude Gothic motifs with vertical mouldings formed by gouged beading near the outer edges of these three boards.

The door is secured to the adjoining side by two large butterfly hinges, and is held closed by a wooden catch fastened to the opposite upright.

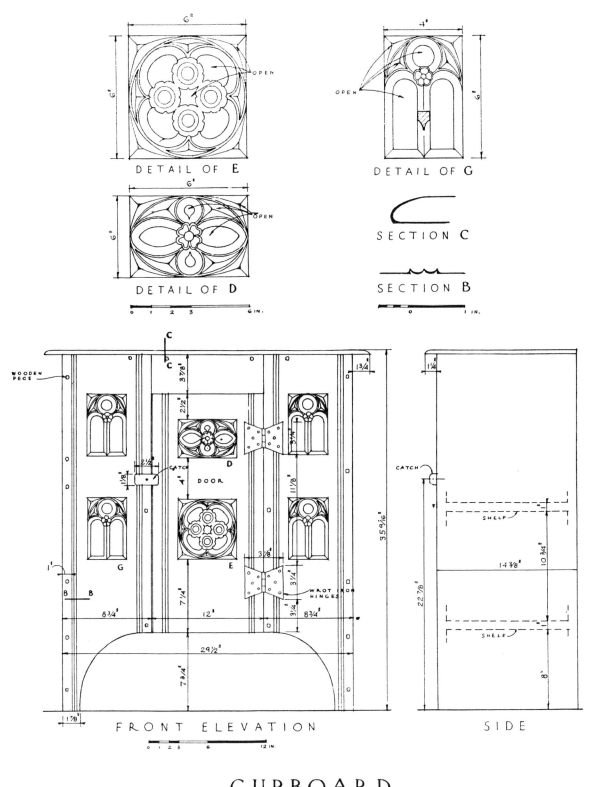

DETAIL OF E

DETAIL OF G

DETAIL OF D

SECTION C

SECTION B

FRONT ELEVATION

SIDE

CUPBOARD
English 15th century (oak)
NOW IN THE METROPOLITAN MUSEUM OF ART

CONNECTICUT CHEST

American 1675-1700

THE accompanying illustration is a fine example of a two-drawer chest of the well known "Connecticut" or "Sun-flower" pattern. Several early chests of this and similar designs were found in Connecticut.

The top is of a single plank of pine, slightly overhanging at the front and back, and fastened to moulded oak cleats at the ends to guide the top and prevent warping. The panelling, of a bold and interesting design, is enriched with round and egg-shaped turtle bosses on the drawer faces and on the upper panel of the ends. Split spindles in various sizes and turnings are applied to the stiles. A horizontal grooved band, frequently found on the chests of this date, decorates the top of the chest between the stiles and appears again between the lower panels of the end.

The carving of the upper panels is in very shallow relief and of a rather crude type—what is known as peasant carving. The central panel represents, it is supposed, three asters, while the outer panels are of a conventionalized tulip.

The woods used in the execution of this chest are both oak and pine. Like most of the similar American-made chests of this date, the top, bottom and backs of both chest and drawers are of pine, the rest of oak.

The bosses, half-spindles, grooves and the main horizontal mouldings are painted black.

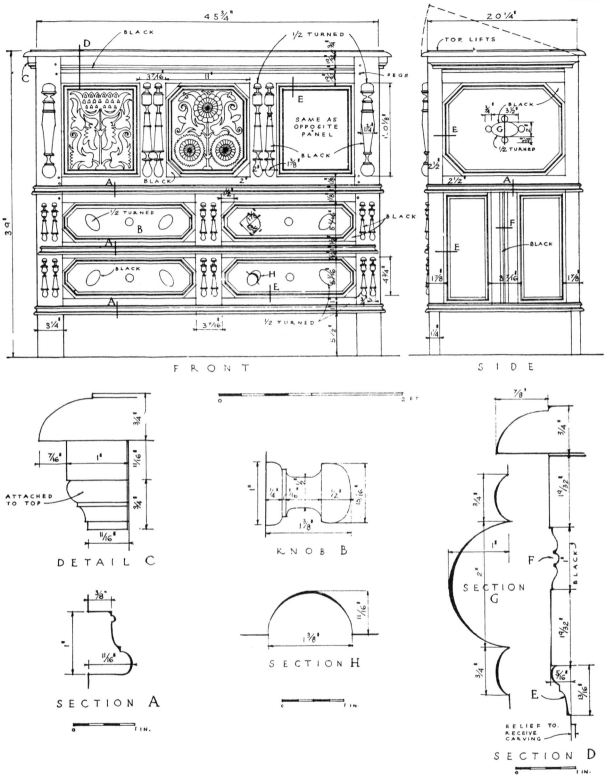

F R O N T

S I D E

DETAIL C

KNOB B

SECTION A

SECTION H

SECTION G

SECTION D

CONNECTICUT CHEST
American about 1675–1700 (of oak)
NOW IN THE METROPOLITAN MUSEUM OF ART

PANELED CHEST

American About 1700

THIS early American paneled chest is of unusual proportions, in that it is extremely high and very narrow. It is constructed with a lifting top disclosing a compartment which occupies about one-third of the entire storage space. The remainder of the chest is occupied by three drawers, which are graduated in width, becoming increasingly wide toward the bottom.

Conforming to the usual custom the lid of this chest is rather thin and is finished at its edges with a thumb moulding. At each end of the carcase, large panels are formed by the structural members, the handles, together with escutcheons, were at that time largely imported from England.

The face of the drawers and compartment above are decorated with a series of panels, simply formed by mouldings. The top compartment is divided into two panels with the upper corners chamfered, and the two upper drawers, ornamented with rectangular and square panels, respectively, while the bottom drawer has those of octagonal shape. A wide single-arch moulding borders each drawer and is mitered into a similar moulding at the stiles. Small ball feet terminate the four prolonged uprights.

The handles are of the brass drop type. These interior edges of the latter being slightly chamfered.

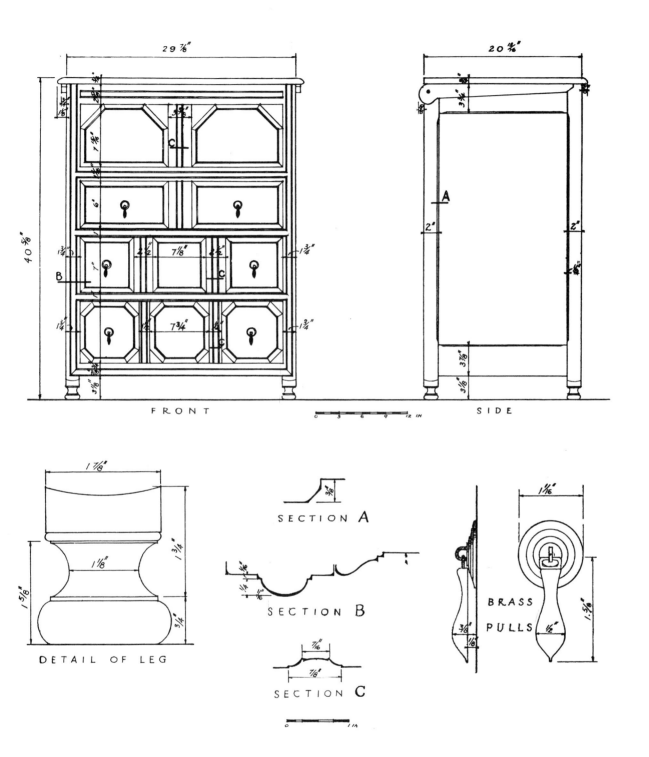

FRONT

SIDE

DETAIL OF LEG

SECTION A

SECTION B

SECTION C

BRASS PULLS

PANELED CHEST
American about 1700 (maple & pine)
NOW IN THE METROPOLITAN MUSEUM OF ART

LOW CHEST OF DRAWERS

Dutch 1725-1750

STRONGLY influenced by Dutch traditions is this low chest of drawers of "kettle" or "bombe" shape. This form was used by Chippendale on some of his best pieces. In America it was also used for chests and desks but only on a limited scale, since the expense of this type of work precluded its greater production.

The top and front of the chest follows the serpentine contour with straight returning sides. Toward the bottom the front as well as the sides swell to a marked degree and return into a lower horizontal moulded member. From this characteristic, that of the swelling frame, is derived the name of "kettle" shape. The four drawer faces, which are cut from solid wood, fill the carcase and con-

form in the swelling and undulating contours to the lines of the framework. Around each drawer, on the frame members, runs a delicate beading.

The piece stands upon four plain squat bandy legs ending in bird's claw and ball feet.

The top is quite thin and somewhat projecting at the sides. It is finished at its edge with a cyma moulding.

The large cabinet mounts are of a type favored by Chippendale and combine strength and delicate grace. Fittings of this type, with certain modifications, were the principal ones used throughout the 18th century. They are composed of a loop handle connected by knobs to a flat shaped plate which was cut in scrolled outline.

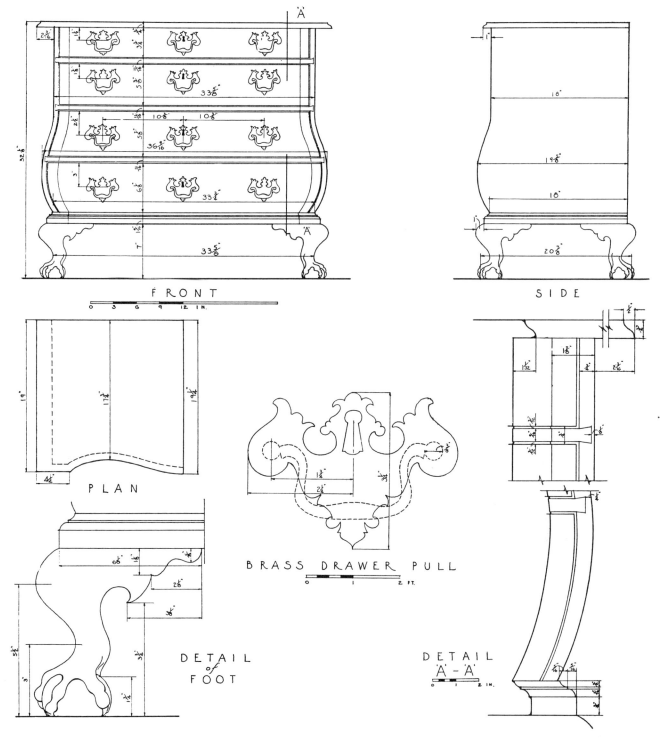

FRONT

SIDE

PLAN

BRASS DRAWER PULL

DETAIL of FOOT

DETAIL 'A'-'A'

LOW CHEST OF DRAWERS
Dutch 1725 - 1750 (Mahogany)

NOW IN THE MUSEUM OF RHODE ISLAND SCHOOL OF DESIGN

CHEST OF DRAWERS

American Circa 1760

THE form of this American chest is based on the serpentine-fronted chests of drawers, fashioned in the later years of the Chippendale period. It is of simple character, severity being redeemed by the shaping of the drawer fronts. This undulation produces an interesting play of light and shade, and also displays to the utmost advantage the rich figure of the mahogany.

The vertical line, produced by the swelling of the front, is carried down through the moulded horizontal member, at the base of the chest, and through the brackets of the legs. The four feet are of the ogee bracket type, ending in flat cushion mouldings at the floor.

Following the customary treatment in chests of the period is the small bead, immediately surrounding each drawer and incorporated on the frame. In the style succeeding, this beading is placed upon the drawer itself, rather than upon the frame work.

The brass mountings are unusual in type for chests following Chippendale inspiration. They recall, rather, those of a later period, being oval in outline. The handles, however, do not extend the full width of the back plate as is general in fittings of later date. The brass is stamped in an ornamental form, and the large escutcheons, which were usually applied to the keyholes, have in this example been omitted.

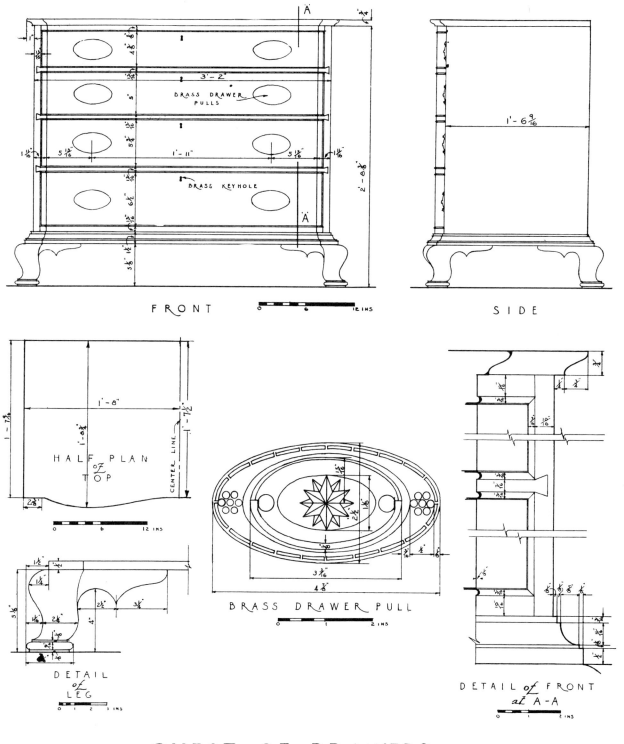

FRONT

SIDE

HALF PLAN of TOP

CENTER LINE

BRASS DRAWER PULL

DETAIL of LEG

DETAIL of FRONT at A-A

BRASS DRAWER PULLS

BRASS KEYHOLE

CHEST OF DRAWERS
American Circa 1760 (Mahogany)
NOW IN THE BOSTON MUSEUM OF FINE ARTS

CHEST OF DRAWERS
American 1790-1800

THIS low chest of drawers with swell front derives its style and traits from Hepplewhite. The lines are chaste, yet not severe, and the main decoration relies upon the rich grain of the inlay and upon the decorative brass handles. The chest rests upon feet of the long French bracket type, a form favored by this designer. The graceful lines of the lower edge join the legs in uninterrupted curves. The framework, of mahogany veneer, contains four drawers, each with two long and one short panel of satinwood inlay, a rectangular panel also being inserted at the skirt. Around the edge of each drawer is a fine bead moulding, a custom made popular by Hepplewhite.

The handles with oval plates which enrich this chest are in the usual form of this period. The plates are of pressed brass handsomely embossed with delicately modelled urns decorated with rams heads, with handles of bails fastened to the outer edge of the posts.

As is the rule with the furniture of the Hepplewhite school, this chest or bureau combines grace and simplicity of line and ornament with the advantage of being "generally serviceable in genteel life" as Hepplewhite himself has said in reference to his own designs.

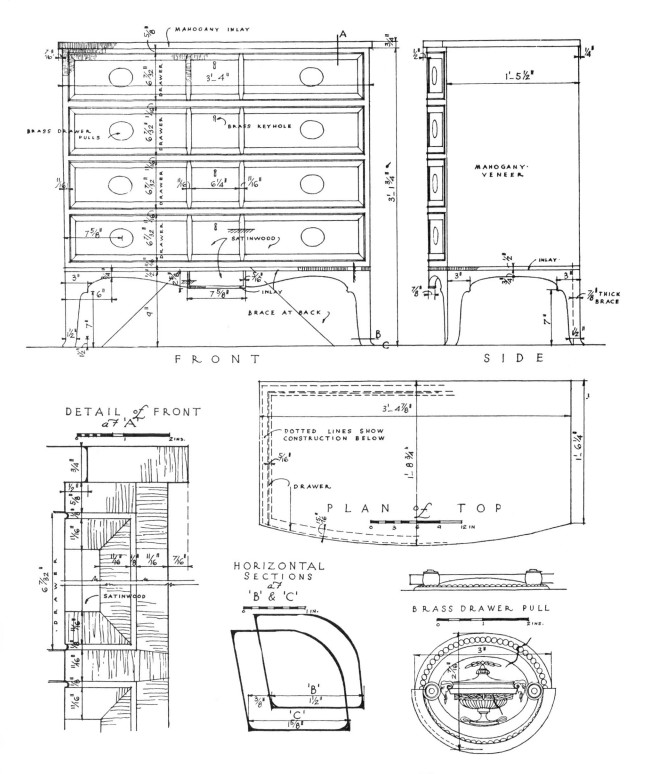

FRONT SIDE

DETAIL of FRONT
at 'A'

PLAN of TOP

HORIZONTAL
SECTIONS
at
'B' & 'C'

BRASS DRAWER PULL

CHEST OF DRAWERS
American 1790-1800 (Mahogany inlaid with Satinwood)
N O W I N T H E M E T R O P O L I T A N M U S E U M O F A R T

BOW-FRONT COMMODE
English

BY THE second quarter of the 18th century, the popularity of the commode had extended, across the channel, to England from France where it had held a position of prestige for some time. The French term "commode" was frequently used by Chippendale, Hepplewhite and Sheraton to designate chests of drawers. Very few pieces of this type, however, were made by American cabinet makers.

In the later years of the 18th century, in England, chests of drawers underwent modifications of form, becoming in many instances semi-circular in shape. Some of these, made by Hepplewhite, were of satinwood and richly inlaid.

The framework of this particular specimen is of mahogany, with four projecting columns extending through the body, which separate the storage space into three compartments, each filled with a series of drawers, veneered with satinwood. The end series, triangular in shape, are hinged at their outer edges, in order that they can swing out from the body.

The top is handsomely inlaid and veneered with radiating strips of satinwood. A charming inlaid design also enriches the front face of the top. The lower portion of the body is finished with a carved waterleaf motif. Lion-mask handles of brass are applied to each drawer. Brass also fashions the animal feet.

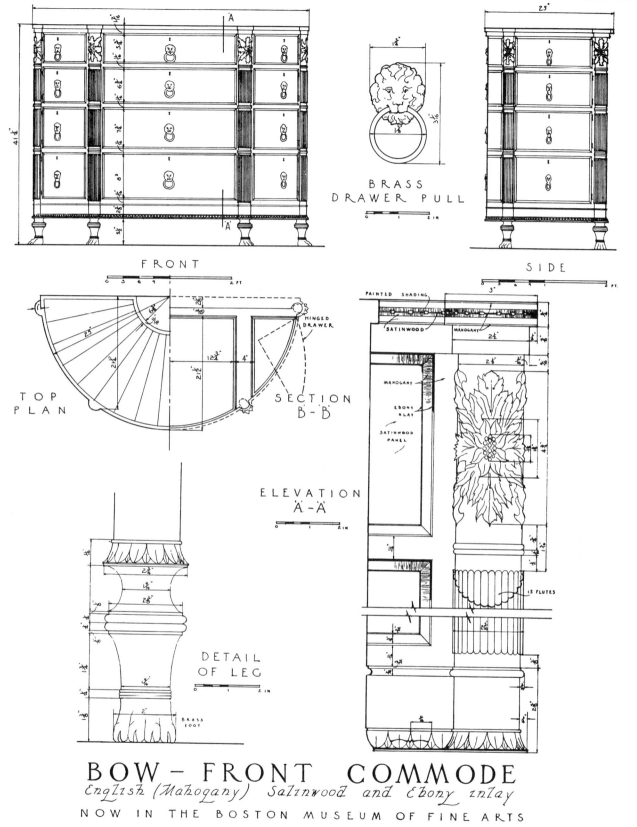

FRONT

SIDE

BRASS
DRAWER PULL

TOP
PLAN

SECTION
B-B

ELEVATION
A-A

DETAIL
OF LEG

BOW – FRONT COMMODE
English (Mahogany) Satinwood and Ebony inlay
NOW IN THE BOSTON MUSEUM OF FINE ARTS

CHEST OF DRAWERS, SHERATON STYLE

American 1800-1825

THIS swell-front mahogany and satinwood bureau is of a rare design. Chests of drawers for use in bedrooms made in the Old World about 1800 were generally bowfronted and sometimes had corners projecting in columns. This specimen follows the dictates of the Sheraton vogue which persisted in fashion in America longer than in England. It represents a transitional phase at the close of the Sheraton influence, rather than the height of that period.

The four corners of the chest are projected in columns all the way to the top of the body and extend below to form the feet. The top is shaped to cover these columns. The upper part of the column, as well as the upper part of the leg, is ornamented with ring turnery, a form of decoration considerably used in the early part of the 19th century.

On the edge of each drawer is a very small bead moulding. The horizontal lines of this beading are repeated by similar and corresponding beading on the corner columns.

Panels of inlaid mahogany and satinwood accent the center of each drawer and incorporate the inlaid pattern around the keyholes.

Round brasses are placed at the extreme ends of the three long drawers and also in the center of the upright drawers which flank the center top compartment.

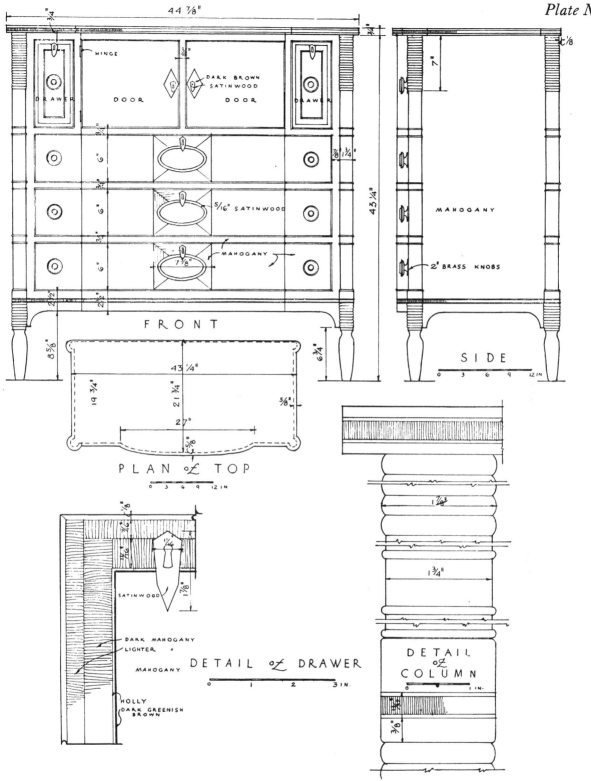

CHEST OF DRAWERS ~ SHERATON STYLE
American 1800-1825 (Mahogany - Satinwood Inlay)
NOW IN THE BOSTON MUSEUM OF FINE ARTS

CABINET, STYLE OF ADAM

English About 1800

CHARACTERISTIC of the introduction of classic features is this cabinet in the style of the brothers Adam. The earlier examples of commodes, following Adelphi influence, were straight-fronted but, after the accession of Louis XVI, the revival of French influence modified and somewhat softened the severity of these rectangular models. In this particular piece of furniture, the contour is governed by the angular element, although the front is slightly bow-shaped. Fluted spade feet, sparingly turned, support the carcase work and the vertical corner supports are seemingly lightened by inlay representing fluting.

The top is made of a slab of pink marble, to which is attached a gallery, cut in an openwork pattern, of brass.

Of marked interest, is the inlaid decoration and the use of vari-colored woods, combined in richly contrasting effects, and, also, the introduction of a few gilded mouldings which accentuate the main structure of the body and reflect the coloring of the brass gallery crowning the top.

The body of this cabinet is of satinwood, a wood popularized by the brothers Adam to such an extent that this period has been often called the "Age of Satinwood."

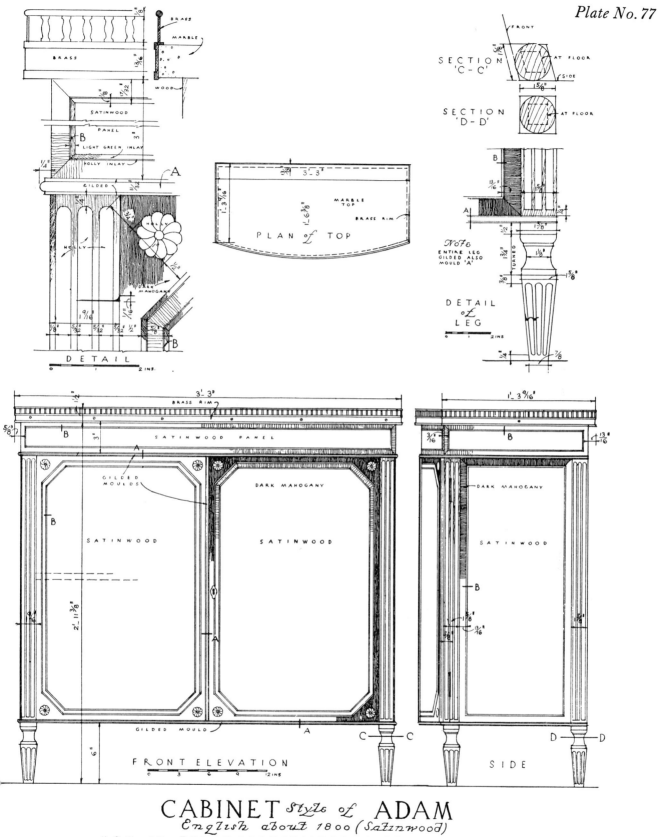

CABINET Style of ADAM

English about 1800 (Satinwood)

NOW IN THE METROPOLITAN MUSEUM OF ART

DESK BOX ON FRAME

American 1650-1700

THIS small desk on a frame, fashioned in colonial America, is an unusual piece of 17th century furniture. It is, in reality, a chest, incorporating a desk-box, superimposed on a long drawer and supported by a structure of four legs, turned and connected by four stretchers of similar character. The front and the sides of the upper portion are ornamented with moulded rectangular panels, divided by a horizontal member, likewise moulded. The structural framework is fastened together by wooden pegs.

Turtle-head bosses, set diagonally, are placed at the center of the upper panels and, in a relative position, on the face of the drawer beneath. The intermediate and end stiles of the front panels are ornamented by the application of split spindles. The use of the latter, with bosses and horizontally grooved mouldings, is representative of this period.

The top, which is finished at its edges with a thumbnail moulding, is hinged to lift, and is provided with wooden guides at each end, which fit against the chest when the top is lowered.

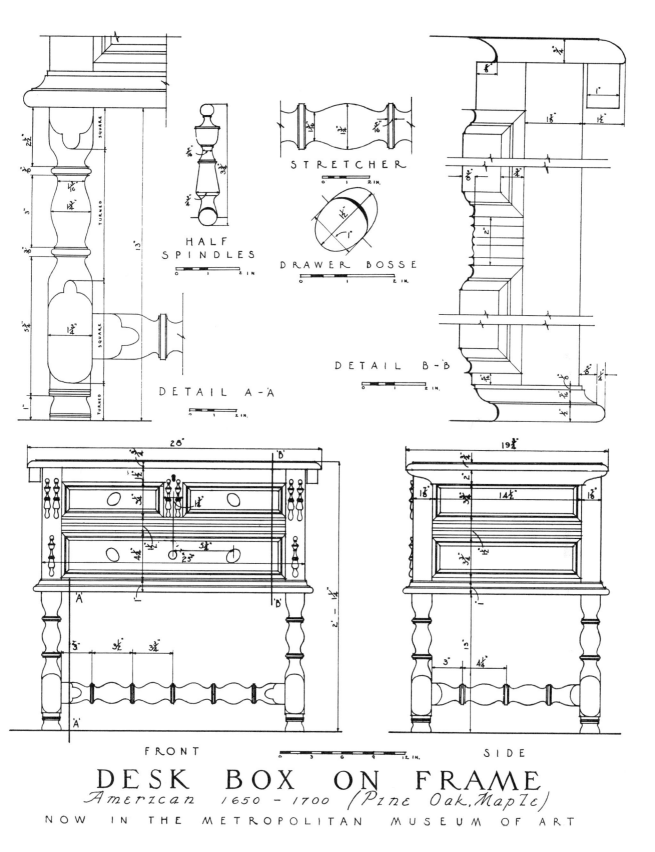

HALF
SPINDLES

STRETCHER

DRAWER BOSSE

DETAIL A-A

DETAIL B-B

FRONT

SIDE

DESK BOX ON FRAME
American 1650 – 1700 (Pine Oak, Maple)
NOW IN THE METROPOLITAN MUSEUM OF ART

WILLIAM AND MARY WRITING CABINET

English About 1700

WRITING became in the early 18th century in England a familiar accomplishment. At this time, cabinet makers were abandoning their strictly ornamental models for the more useful types, and we consequently find, among the articles of early 18th century furniture, pieces called "scrutoires" or writing cabinets.

This specimen is of English origin, very few examples modeled after this fashion having been produced in our colonies.

It is composed of two superimposed carcases, the upper, consisting of a solid front concealing drawers and pigeon holes, while the lower contains two large drawers below two shorter ones at the top. Surrounding these drawers and a part of the frame is a single arch-moulding. The base of the carcase is finished with a moulding of flaring outline and the whole is supported upon four ball-turned feet.

The upper portion is topped with a cornice, showing classical influence and incorporating a frieze of half-round or cushion shape—an architectural mannerism dating from the late years of the 17th and the first years of the 18th centuries. A veneered rectangular panel enriches the fall at the front of the upper case.

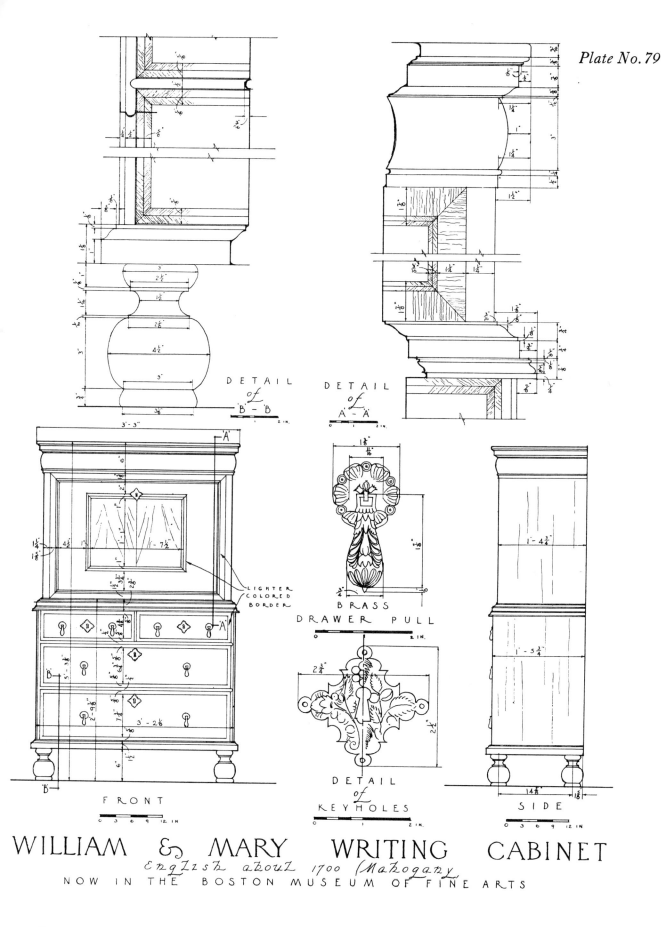

DETAIL
of
B - B

DETAIL
of
A - A

BRASS
DRAWER PULL

DETAIL
of
KEYHOLES

LIGHTER
COLORED
BORDER

FRONT

SIDE

WILLIAM & MARY WRITING CABINET

English about 1700 (Mahogany

NOW IN THE BOSTON MUSEUM OF FINE ARTS

SLANT TOP DESK
American Early XVIII Century

AN AMERICAN scrutoire closely following the pattern of the lower chest of the William and Mary writing cabinet, Plate 79, is pictured here. It incorporates the major characteristics of the desks of this period (1700-1710).

Below the desk top, which is a development of the movable desk-box, is provided a series of drawers raised on large spherical feet. A double bead moulding ornaments the vertical and horizontal members of the drawer framework and is also extended up the slanting frame at the flap. The flaring moulding at the bottom of the desk body is typical of this style.

The slant-top, when lowered, rests upon small wooden slides, placed in the box-like portion above the two top drawers. The fittings, inside the desk, comprise a central space, flanked at either end by a gradually projecting arrangement of pigeon-holes and drawers.

Characteristic of this period, is the large ball type foot. This example, however, differs somewhat from the usual form, in that it rests upon a flaring shoe.

The body of the desk is beautifully veneered. Double bandings of herringbone, in burled walnut, border the veneered panels of the drawers.

The brass handles are of the drop type, and large etched key escutcheons offset, by contrast, the rich surface of the wood.

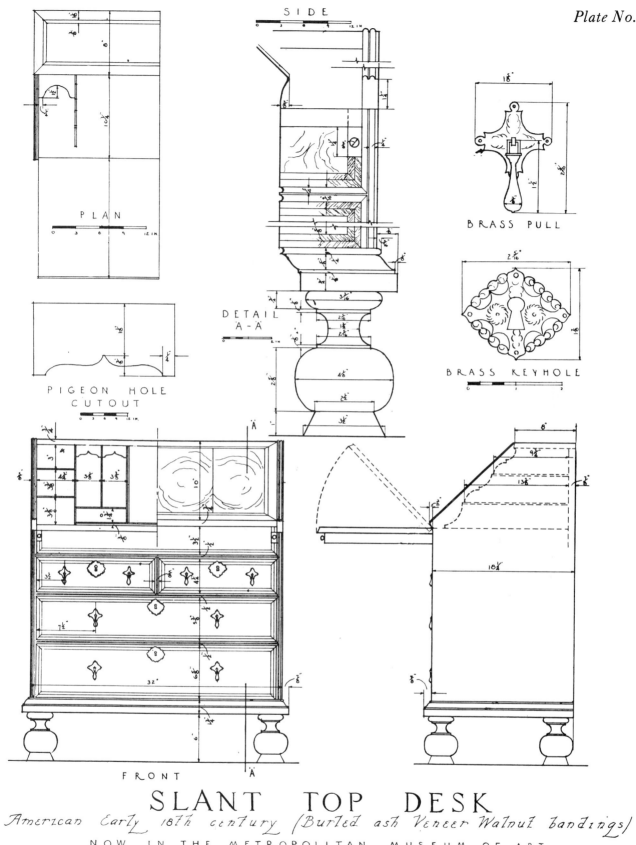

PLAN

SIDE

DETAIL
'A - A'

PIGEON HOLE
CUTOUT

BRASS PULL

BRASS KEYHOLE

FRONT

SLANT TOP DESK

American Early 18th century (Burled ash Veneer Walnut bandings)

NOW IN THE METROPOLITAN MUSEUM OF ART

KNEE HOLE DESK
English XVIII Century

ONE of the early types of desk or dressing tables was made in the form shown by this illustration. The central portion is recessed to allow the user to sit snugly and comfortably at the desk or dressing table. The name "knee hole" was evidently derived from the cutting away of this central portion.

On each side of the center are drawers and in the recess is built a cupboard, which served the needs of the desk as well as those of the dressing table.

In similar pieces, designed solely as a desk, a change appears in the construction of the top drawer. The front is frequently made to fall on a quadrant, forming a surface upon which to write. Within, the desk is fitted with pigeon-holes and drawers.

However, this piece of furniture was as frequently made to support a dressing-glass, in which case, the top compartment appeared in the form of a drawer.

In the example, the front part of the drawers are of walnut veneer, bordered with edges of herringbone. This herringbone treatment was a favorite method of early inlaid decoration.

The feet are of the later bracket type, and the cut-work bracket, which forms the corners of the recess, indicate Chinese influence. Also, of a later period, are the brass mountings, of a decidedly French feeling.

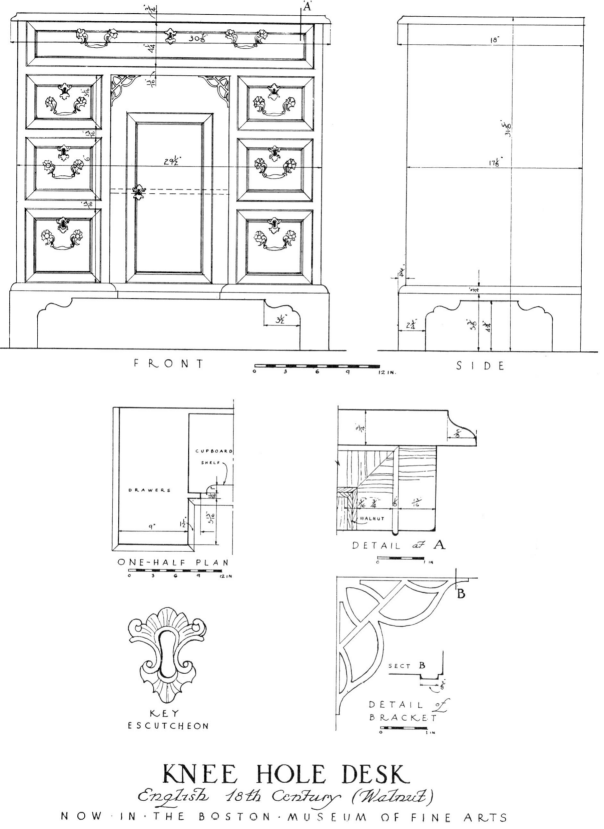

FRONT

0 3 6 9 12 IN.

SIDE

ONE-HALF PLAN

0 3 6 9 12 IN

CUPBOARD
SHELF

DRAWERS

DETAIL of A

0 1 IN

B

SECT B

DETAIL of
BRACKET

0 1 IN

KEY
ESCUTCHEON

WALNUT

KNEE HOLE DESK
English 18th Century (Walnut)
NOW · IN · THE · BOSTON · MUSEUM · OF · FINE · ARTS

TAMBOUR DESK, STYLE OF HEPPLEWHITE

American About 1780-1810

CHARMING in design and delightfully fulfilling the requirements of the writing cabinet is this desk, a variation of the Hepplewhite style.

The lower section comprises two long drawers, below a flap top which folds over double. When extended, this flap rests upon two wooden slides, placed at the ends of the upper drawers. Supporting the body are four slender, tapering legs, the front two being connected with a deep apron, cut to a gracefully curving outline.

Above the flap, the top compartment is concealed behind tambour doors. These are composed of narrow beaded strips of wood, glued side by side to a stiff canvas backing. These strips are attached to inlaid vertical members, forming center stiles. The tambour door was a form of decorative construction used in the late 18th century. Behind these doors are revealed pigeon-holes and a series of small drawers.

An interesting motif of inlaid decoration appears on the upright members of the desk top and is placed upon the body portion of the legs. This design, representing a classic pilaster, is made up of very narrow bands of light colored inlay. Also panels of inlay, with varying borders of intricately inlaid patterns, ornament the central portion of the two large drawers.

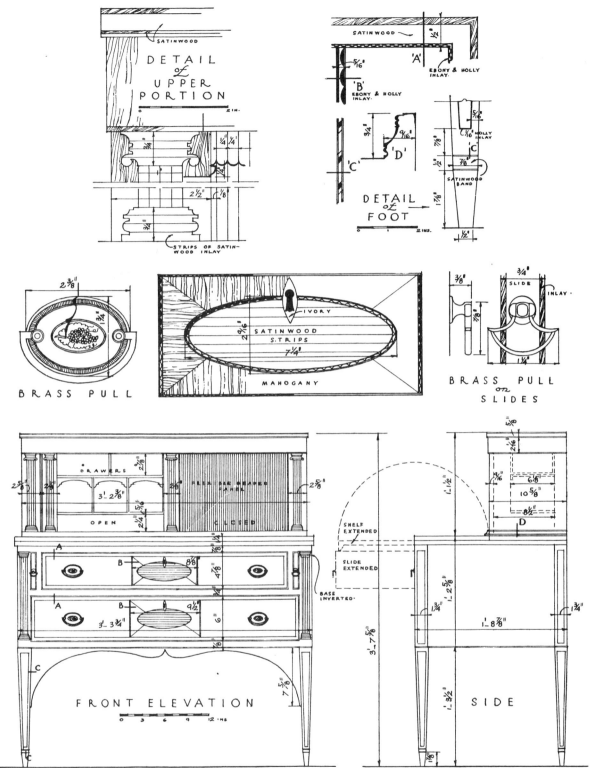

DETAIL
of
UPPER
PORTION

SATINWOOD

STRIPS OF SATIN-
WOOD INLAY

DETAIL
of
FOOT

EBONY & HOLLY
INLAY.

EBONY & HOLLY
INLAY.

HOLLY
INLAY.

SATINWOOD
BAND

BRASS PULL

IVORY

SATINWOOD
S. STRIPS

MAHOGANY

BRASS PULL
on
SLIDES

SLIDE
INLAY.

DRAWERS

OPEN   CLOSED

FLEXIBLE REEDED PANEL

SHELF
EXTENDED

SLIDE
EXTENDED

BASE
INVERTED

FRONT ELEVATION

0 3 6 9   12 INS.

SIDE

TAMBOUR DESK *Style of* HEPPLEWHITE
American about 1780-1810 (Mahogany and Satinwood)
NOW IN THE METROPOLITAN MUSEUM OF ART

DESK, STYLE OF SHERATON

American About 1800

AN unusual piece of furniture is this tiny "Lady's Writing Desk" of Sheraton conception. In nicety of proportion and slenderized construction it is a noteworthy exponent of this style.

It is fashioned of mahogany, with maple door and with this light colored wood also applied to the panels of the body framework.

The stand upon which the desk rests is of the shape of a small table supported upon four slender, reeded legs of mahogany, with ring turnings at the top and ankle, and finished at the foot with casters of brass.

A small single drawer is fitted into the stand and is provided with two handsome brass pulls.

The movable box-like desk, with brass handles attached at the sides for lifting is set on the rear of the table, so that when the door flap is lowered it rests in a slanting position, against the front of the table top.

Drawers, fitted with very small brass knobs and a central pigeon-hole, make up the arrangement of the interior of the desk.

Inlaid bands, of a rather rich pattern, border the maple panels and also run down the middle of the desk flap, giving the latter the appearance of being two side-hinged doors.

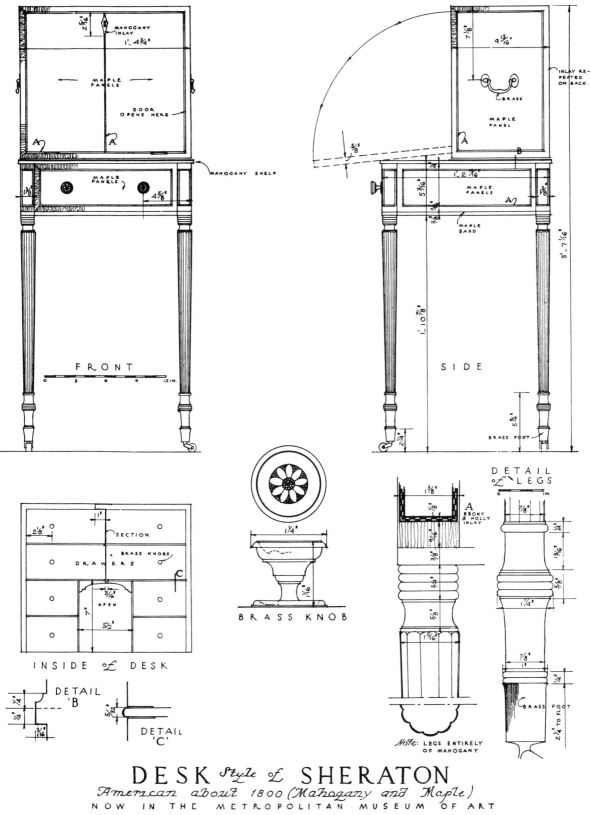

MAHOGANY INLAY
1'-4¾"
2⁹⁄₁₆

MAPLE PANELS
DOOR OPENS HERE
A
A
MAHOGANY SHELF

MAPLE PANELS
1⅜"
4⅝"

FRONT
0   3   6   9   12 IN.

7⅞"
9¹³⁄₁₆
BRASS
MAPLE PANEL
INLAY REPEATED ON BACK
A
B
5⁄₈"
5⁄₁₆"
1'-2⁷⁄₁₆"
MAPLE PANELS
A
MAPLE BAND
3⁄₁₆"
1⅛"
3'-7⁷⁄₁₆"
1'-10⅞"

SIDE
5⅝"
2¼"
BRASS FOOT

SECTION
1"
2½"
BRASS KNOBS
DRAWERS
C
3⁄₁₆"
OPEN
7"
5½"

INSIDE ⅃ DESK

DETAIL 'B'
¼"
¼"
½"
3⁄₁₆"

DETAIL 'C'
5⁄₃₂"

1¼"
1⁄₁₆"
BRASS KNOB

DETAIL ⅃ LEGS
0   ½   1 IN.
7⁄₈"
¼"
1³⁄₁₆"
5⁄₈"
1¼"
7⁄₈"
1"
¼"
BRASS FOOT
2¼" TO FLOT

1⅜"
⅛"
A
EBONY & HOLLY INLAY
9⁄₁₆"
3⁄₈"
¾"
5⁄₈"
1⁵⁄₁₆"

Note: LEGS ENTIRELY OF MAHOGANY

DESK *Style of* SHERATON
American about 1800 (Mahogany and Maple)
NOW IN THE METROPOLITAN MUSEUM OF ART

VARGUEÑO

Spanish XVI Century

VARGUEÑO cabinets exemplified the highest attainments of the Spanish cabinet makers. In skilful construction and in mastery of the art of decoration, they are distinctly characteristic of Spanish furniture, which, in this art, reached the highest point of excellence.

These pieces of furniture were habitually made of walnut, a wood which lent itself to ornate turning and carving. At times, inlay, as well as color, was added to heighten the effect.

The vargueño consists of a chest, which rests upon a stand made expressly for this cabinet, but which was treated in a decorative manner quite different from the cabinet it supported.

In this special example, the stand is made up of three legs at each end, which rise from a runner foot and support above a heavy cross rail upon which the cabinet rests. From these block rail braces, two massive supports pull out to hold the drop front when the latter is lowered. These slides are ornamented on their exposed ends with the cockle shell motif, carved in high relief. An arcaded stretcher, richly turned; connects the center leg supports.

The exterior of the chest itself is of the simplest nature, depending for decorative effect upon the handsome and intricate designs of the applied ironwork. In Spain metal trimmings were developed to an extraordinary degree and far excelled this craft in other parts of Europe.

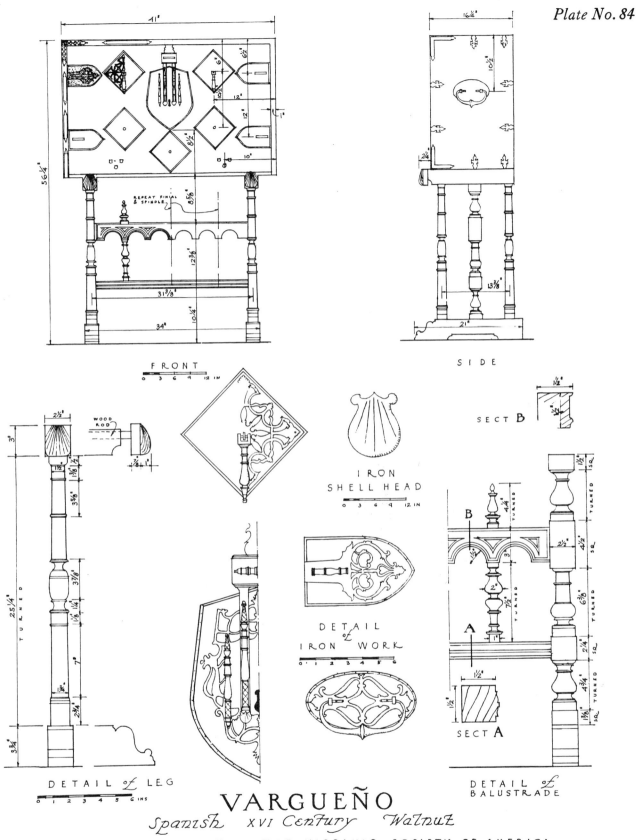

Plate No. 84

FRONT

0 3 6 9 12 IN

SIDE

SECT B

WOOD
ROD

IRON
SHELL HEAD

0 3 6 9 12 IN

DETAIL
of
IRON WORK

0 1 2 3 4 5 6

B

A

SECT A

DETAIL of LEG

0 1 2 3 4 5 6 INS

DETAIL of
BALUSTRADE

VARGUEÑO
Spanish XVI Century Walnut

NOW IN THE MUSEUM OF THE HISPANIC SOCIETY OF AMERICA

QUEEN ANNE SECRETARY
English Early XVII Century

THIS walnut secretary with its high and rectangular construction is typical of the more simple types of Queen Anne cabinets. Bureaux in two stages, with the upper structure placed upon the narrow shelf above the desk portion, appeared at that time since the increased height of rooms then being built demanded furniture of greater stature.

A feature, exceedingly characteristic of the furniture of this period, is the hooded top. Sometimes, a single hood was fancied but, more often, the hood with the double dome as illustrated in the accompanying example was favored.

The glass of the doors is outlined with a semicircular moulding, which, at the top, is scrolled in an interesting hooded effect that conforms to, and accentuates, in a delightful manner, the cornice above. Shelves are fitted into the compartment behind. Below are two small drawers, each cut in a double concave outline and bordered with double bands of walnut inlay.

The desk with falling front, operated by a quadrant, is situated in the lower portion. Below it is a series of drawers, supported upon simple bracket feet.

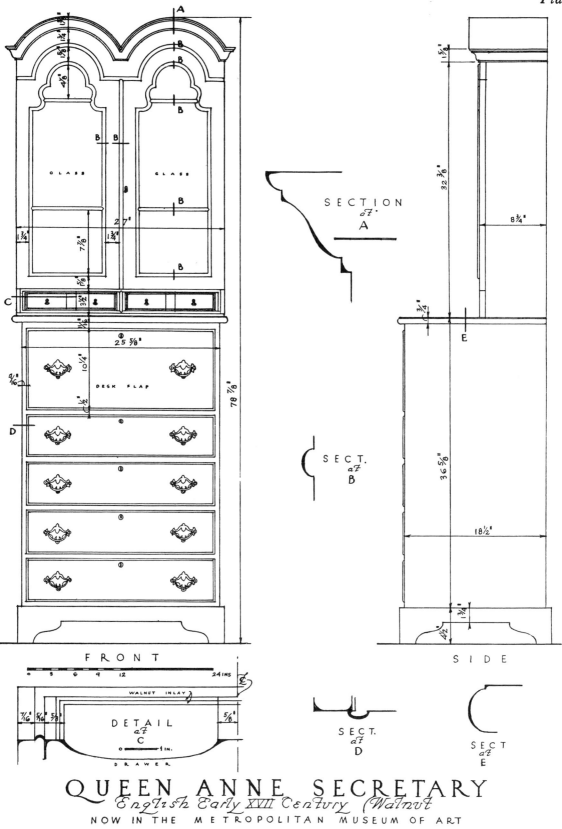

SECTION of A

SECT. at B

SIDE

SECTION of A

FRONT

DETAIL at C

DRAWER

WALNUT INLAY

SECT. at D

SECT at E

GLASS   GLASS

DESK FLAP

QUEEN ANNE SECRETARY
English Early XVII Century Walnut
NOW IN THE METROPOLITAN MUSEUM OF ART

AMERICAN SECRETARY
1765-1780

THE third quarter of the 18th century, in America, as well as in France and England, was one of the most brilliant in the history of furniture design. During this period, secretaries, particularly those with a slant top desk, enjoyed their greatest popularity.

The example under discussion follows Chippendale prototypes and embodies many features favored at this time, one of which was the hooded and scrolled top. In New England this feature was generally enclosed, as we find it here, whereas, in specimens of Southern origin, the lines of the ogee broken arch at the front were not, as a rule, carried back but left a flat top, behind this ornamental motif.

The lower or desk section contains, below the slant top, drawers of ox bow shape. The whole carcase is supported upon feet of ogee bracket type.

Two large doors are provided in the upper section or bookcase top. These doors are ornamented with sunken panels whose outlines are composed of a series of cyma curves.

The fluted pilasters and denticulated cornice, together with the scroll top, show the influence of the architectural backgrounds in which such pieces of furniture were placed. The finials, surmounting the pilaster treatment and between the rosetted scrolls, are of urn shape, terminating in a flame motif.

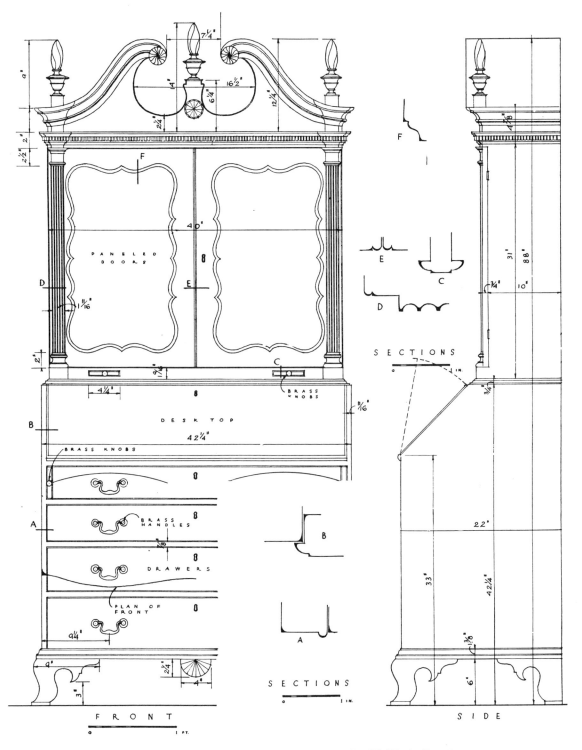

AMERICAN SECRETARY
Mahogany 1765-1780
NOW IN THE METROPOLITAN MUSEUM OF ART

BLOCK-FRONT SECRETARY
American 1750-1775

THIS block-front, cabinet-top scrutoire, is attributed to John Goddard, an 18th century cabinet maker of Newport, Rhode Island, who executed some of the finest pieces of American furniture.

The top is scrolled and hooded, its crowning moulding returning at the inner ends of the scrolls and the lower moulded members of the cornice carried around the circular opening. This latter treatment is seldom, if ever, found outside of Rhode Island pieces.

Inserted in the corners of the upper portion are quarter round fluted columns, partially reeded. Between are three doors of high, perpendicular proportions. Two of these are hinged together. The panels of the outer doors are raised and headed with carved shells, whereas the center one is depressed with its shell design, similar in form to those adjacent but of sunken relief.

In the lower portion the slanting desk lid is blocked with a repetition of the raised and sunken panels, ending at their tops in carved shells. The chest below is again blocked with the blocking carried down through the three drawers to the ogee feet.

Three finials of urn and flame pattern, distinctly characteristic of Rhode Island pieces, grace the top of the hood.

The interior of the desk is fitted with pigeonholes and drawers which flank the central door. A carved shell motif is used to enrich the top of this door as well as the two small upper drawers.

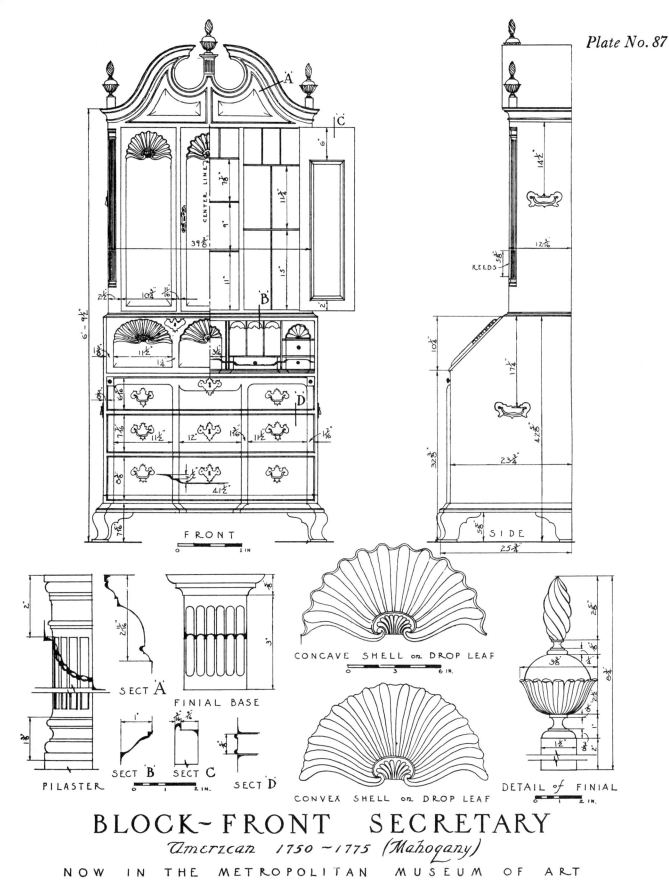

FRONT

SIDE

REEDS

CONCAVE SHELL on DROP LEAF

CONVEX SHELL on DROP LEAF

SECT 'A'

FINIAL BASE

SECT 'B' SECT C

SECT 'D'

PILASTER

DETAIL of FINIAL

BLOCK~FRONT SECRETARY
American 1750 ~ 1775 (Mahogany)
NOW IN THE METROPOLITAN MUSEUM OF ART

SHERATON STYLE BOOKCASE-TOP DESK
American 1790-1800

EMBODYING many of the characteristic features of bookcases, following the patterns prescribed by Sheraton, is this particular example. Of imposing proportions, it comprises drawers and cupboard doors, in the lower portion, upon which rests the bookcase top. Sheraton's patterns frequently, as in this example, were made in three sections, with the middle portion projecting beyond the flanking sections. It was also a characteristic feature for the upper portion to be somewhat receded from the unit below.

The four bookcase doors are glazed and traceried in a geometric design.

The peg-top foot is indicative of the majority of late pieces of Sheraton influence. In the outline of the cresting, which tops the upper portion of the carcase work, the curvilinear is introduced. It is broken at its points of vertical support and at the center, by finial terminations of delicate urn-shaped turnings.

In this example inlay is introduced only on the four front faces of the leg supports which are carried up through the lower unit. Oval brass drawer fittings give needed contrast to this impressive bookcase-top desk which is executed entirely of mahogany.

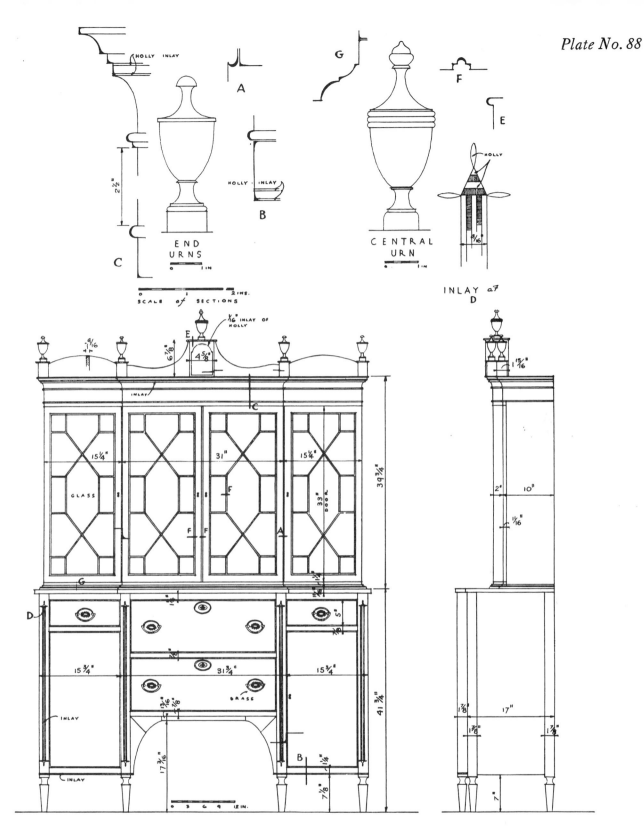

HOLLY INLAY

A

B

C

HOLLY INLAY

END
URNS

G

F

E

HOLLY

CENTRAL
URN

INLAY at
D

SCALE of SECTIONS

INLAY

GLASS

F

F F A

G

D

INLAY

INLAY

BRASS

B

SHERATON STYLE BOOKCASE-TOP DESK
American 1790-1800 (Mahogany)
NOW IN THE METROPOLITAN MUSEUM OF ART

STRAIGHT-FRONT SECRETARY

American About 1807

CONFORMING in the essentials to the vogue of the time is this straight-front secretary which dates from the early years of the 19th century. It has been attributed to Appleton of Salem.

The carcase is built in two sections. A movable bookcase top rests upon a desk. The bookcase portion is fitted with shelves behind glazed doors, whose muntins are diagonally placed, forming a geometric pattern. The front of the upper compartment in the lower section falls, disclosing a desk. Below are three drawers, all of which are outlined with a delicate bead moulding. The piece stands on long French bracket feet—a typical Hepplewhite detail—which are connected by an apron of graceful serpentine outline.

Crowning the bookcase is a denticulated cornice, topped with curved cresting, terminating at the corners in delicate blocks supporting brass finials.

The cresting rises at the center to receive a large carved "spread eagle." This national emblem was a popular motif of decoration during the early days of the Republic, and was frequently used in inlay as well as in relief. It was also adopted by workers in brass, principally, as a motif on drawer pulls. The oval shaped brasses are almost without exception found upon furniture following Hepplewhite's models containing drawers.

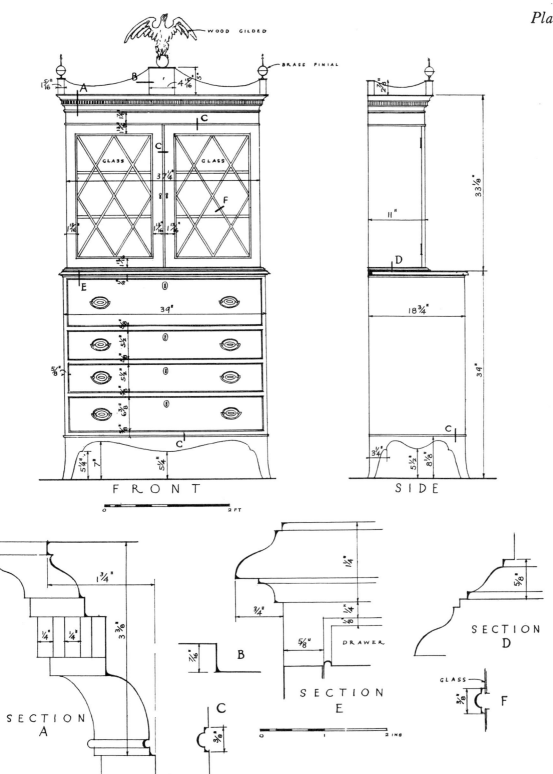

WOOD GILDED

BRASS FINIAL

A

B

C

GLASS GLASS

C

F

37¼"

E

39"

5½"

5½"

6⅜"

FRONT

0   2 FT

SIDE

7⅜"

11"

D

33⅛"

18¾"

34"

C

3¾"

5½"

8⅛"

SECTION A

1¾"

3⅜"

¼" ¼"

7/16"

B

C

3/8"

¼"

¾"

¼"

1/80

5/8"

DRAWER

SECTION E

0   1   2 INS

SECTION D

5/8"

GLASS

3/8"

F

STRAIGHT-FRONT SECRETARY
American Made by Appleton of Salem about 1807
NOW IN THE ESSEX INSTITUTE SALEM MASS

PAINTED HIGHBOY

American 1680-1700

A TYPE of the earliest development of the American highboy, a combination of the chest of drawers and table, is shown here. The six legs are elaborately turned, the four at the front in a cup-shaped pattern, while the two back legs are of more slender form. They are braced near the floor on the front and sides with a thin, broad stretcher, slightly curved inwards, and across the back with a stretcher placed vertically and cut in a quaint design of large scallops.

This piece of furniture is constructed in two sections, the lower containing two panelled drawers. In the upper portion are five drawers of varying widths which operate on side runners, while the two drawers beneath have one runner at the side and another at the bottom. A single arch moulding, common to highboys of this early period, finishes the frame about the upper set of drawers and is repeated on the stiles of the lower section. The stiles and rails of the frame are mortised and tenoned.

The main body of the highboy is painted black, relieved by bands of red, a very striking combination. The large raised panels of the ends are picked out in red.

The brass drawer pulls are of the drop style with engraved plates of charming design. The brass key escutcheons are of a cut-out pattern.

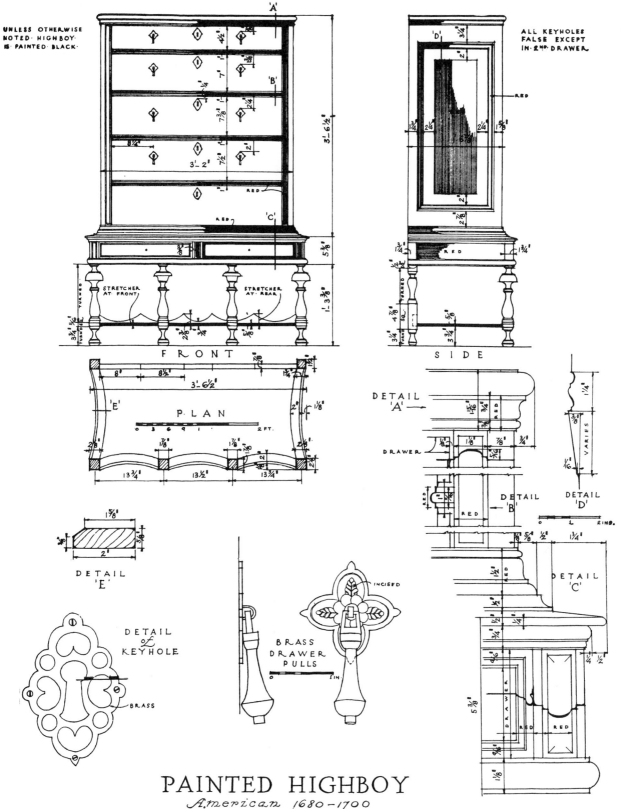

UNLESS OTHERWISE
NOTED HIGHBOY
IS PAINTED BLACK

ALL KEYHOLES
FALSE EXCEPT
IN 2ND DRAWER

FRONT

SIDE

PLAN

DETAIL 'A'

DRAWER

DETAIL 'B'

DETAIL 'D'

DETAIL 'E'

DETAIL of KEYHOLE

BRASS

BRASS DRAWER PULLS

INCISED

DETAIL 'C'

PAINTED HIGHBOY
American 1680–1700
NOW IN THE METROPOLITAN MUSEUM OF ART

WALNUT HIGHBOY

American 1700-1710

THIS walnut highboy, made in America very early in the 18th century, follows the William and Mary precedent. The highboy remained in favor many years longer in America than in England and was made here in greater numbers.

The "highboy," a name of American origin, usually consists, as is represented by this piece, of a chest of drawers, supported by a five or six-legged stand, embracing a few drawers and with a shaped apron, connecting the legs immediately above the feet. The upper portion or chest was, as a rule, four drawers high with the upper one divided into two or three smaller drawers.

On the framework surrounding these drawers is a double bead moulding. At this time, this type of moulding shared, for this particular treatment, favor with one of half round contour.

The six legs of this stand are of the inverted cup type, typical of the William and Mary period. The legs are connected above the bun-shaped feet with flat stretchers which are shaped to a concave outline between the two intermediate legs and follow the ogee pattern elsewhere.

The lower edge of the skirt is cut to a contour of cyma curves and, at its center, a single arch is introduced.

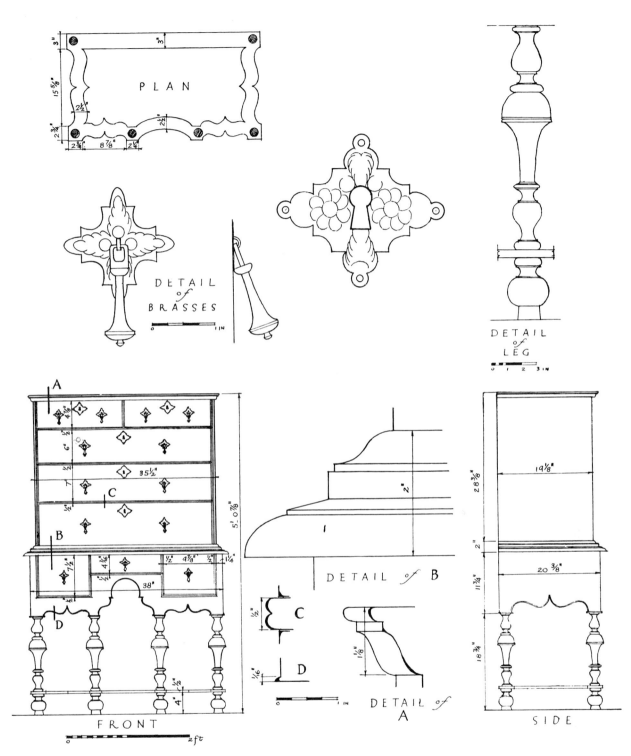

PLAN

DETAIL of BRASSES

DETAIL of LEG

A

B

C

D

FRONT

2ft

DETAIL of B

DETAIL of A

C

D

SIDE

WALNUT HIGHBOY
American · 1700 – 1710
NOW · IN · THE · METROPOLITAN MUSEUM OF ART.

LACQUERED HIGHBOY

1700-1725

AN INTERESTING japanned high chest of drawers is shown here. In the last few years of the 17th century the art of japanning, imported from the Orient, became exceedingly popular in Europe, and the fad consequently extended to the American colonies. At times the decoration was in color, but, as is shown in this example, the general custom was to build up the decoration with plaster and apply gilding. The designs on the drawers are in the Oriental character with flowers, houses, figures and animals freely scattered but invariably forming a well balanced composition. A large shell fills the circular recess in the lower, central drawer and is flanked with raised columns.

In the early 18th century the American highboy followed the popular fashion and adopted the bandy or cabriole leg. The cutting of the skirt is typical of the period, as is the narrow beading about the drawers of both the upper and lower portions.

The brass handles belong to a later type of highboy. They consist of a bail handle fastened to an exquisitely engraved plate. The key escutcheons are of different designs but similar in character.

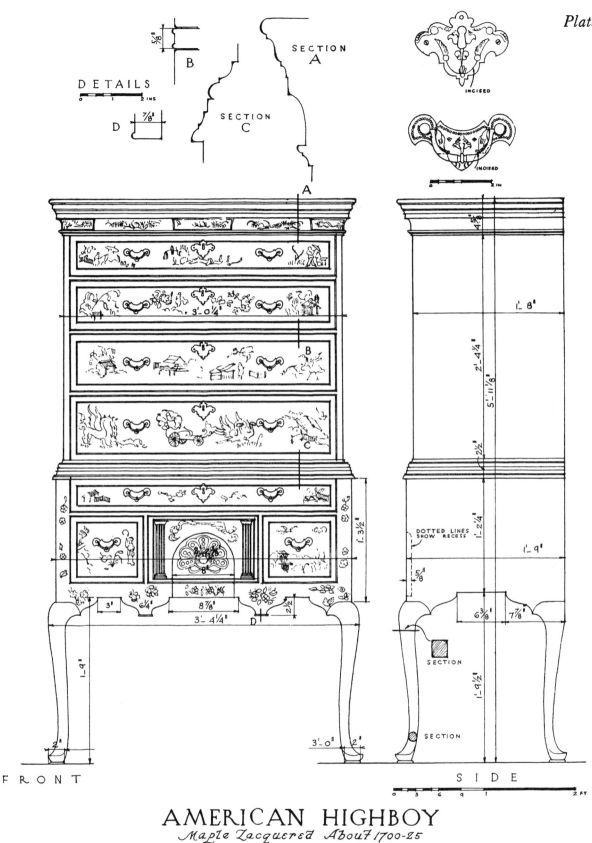

SECTION A

SECTION C

SECTION B

DETAILS

INCISED

INCISED

FRONT

SIDE

DOTTED LINES SHOW RECESS

SECTION

SECTION

AMERICAN HIGHBOY
Maple Lacquered About 1700-25
NOW IN THE METROPOLITAN MUSEUM OF ART

HIGHBOY

American 1725-1750

THE highboy enjoyed a greater development in America than abroad where its popularity was rather limited. In England as well as on the continent their position was taken by commodes whose vogue, commencing in France, soon received generous support in England. In America, however, the highboy held position in the public esteem that was unassailable until the end of the 18th century. Until about 1750 walnut was the wood preferred for the construction of these "chests of drawers on stand," as the highboy was frequently called, as well as for all other pieces of furniture with pretentions to elegance. After that date the use of mahogany increased in favor and rapidly supplanted the native woods.

The example under discussion is surmounted by an interrupted pediment of scroll form. In the middle of this pediment and repeated at each end are turned finials of urn shape with long, spiral flames. Finishing each stile and framing a series of drawers are delicately fluted pilasters of classic form which carry through the cornice.

The stand is supported upon cabriole legs of an early form, which are connected by a skirt cut in a design of quarter circles separated by straight lines from which hang small turned pendants.

The top and lower central drawers are decorated with large carved motifs—that of the rising sun. The carving of this pattern, as well as the turning and carving of the finials and the execution of the mouldings, is executed in a well defined manner.

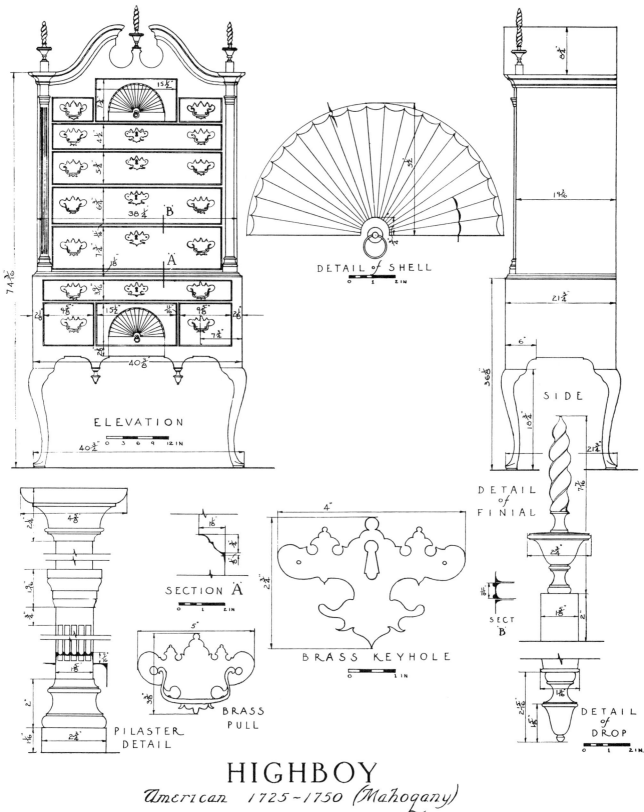

DETAIL of SHELL

ELEVATION

SIDE

DETAIL of FINIAL

SECTION A

BRASS KEYHOLE

SECT B

BRASS PULL

PILASTER DETAIL

DETAIL of DROP

HIGHBOY

American 1725~1750 (Mahogany)

NOW IN THE METROPOLITAN MUSEUM OF ART

BED WITH TESTER RAILS

American 1790-1800

AFTER the middle of the 18th century, four-post bedsteads became much lighter in form. Their predecessors of the 16th, 17th and early years of the 18th centuries were of a much more ponderous character. These later specimens, however, continued to be handsomely carved and were still richly draped.

It was the custom to expose only the two front posts and the cornice, the remainder of the bedstead being draped in such a manner as to conceal the other members. This fashion accounts for the simplicity and lack of ornamentation of the portions of the bedstead not readily visible in comparison with the ornateness of those parts which are directly exposed. The necking of the front posts regulated the depth of the valance which hung from the tester rail.

The front posts above the black are bulb turned and reeded, with the turnings immediately below richly carved with beadings, egg and dart mouldings, and conventionalized acanthus leaf motifs. The head posts are plain and tapered with corners chamfered. Brass rosettes cover the bolt holes.

In contrast with the mahogany of the posts is the tester rail of pine. The latter is painted a cream color with blue stripings. Interesting motifs composed of musical instruments combined with foliage are painted upon the center and corner panels.

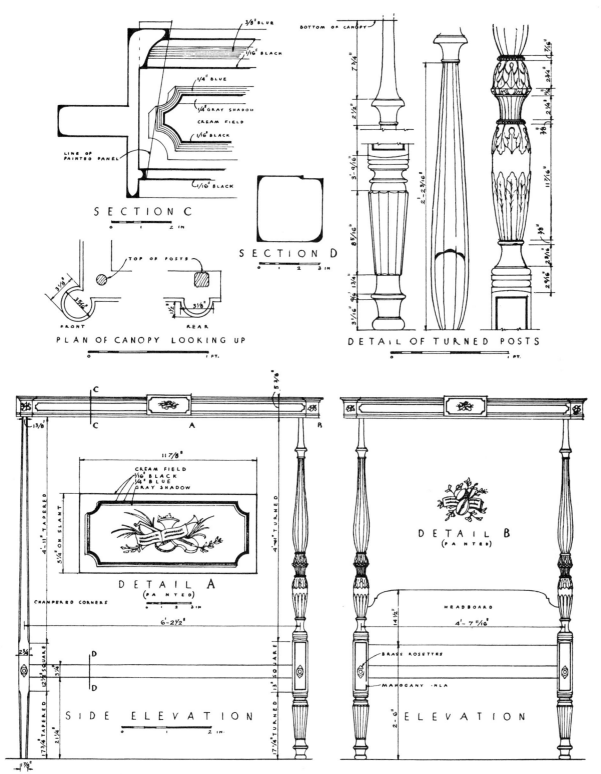

SECTION C

3/8" BLUE
1/16" BLACK
1/4" BLUE
1/4" GRAY SHADOW
CREAM FIELD
1/16" BLACK
LINE OF PAINTED PANEL
1/16" BLACK

SECTION D

BOTTOM OF CANOPY

TOP OF POSTS

FRONT   REAR

PLAN OF CANOPY LOOKING UP

DETAIL OF TURNED POSTS

CREAM FIELD
1/16" BLACK
1/4" BLUE
GRAY SHADOW

11 7/8"

DETAIL A
(PAINTED)

4'-11" TAPERED
5 1/4" ON SLANT
4'-11" TURNED

CHAMPERED CORNERS

6'-2 1/2"

SIDE ELEVATION

D   D

12 1/2" SQUARE
13" TURNED

17 3/4" TAPERED
2 1/4"
17 1/4" TURNED

DETAIL B
(PAINTED)

HEADBOARD
4'-7 11/16"

14 1/2"

BRASS ROSETTES

MAHOGANY INLA

2'-6"   ELEVATION

BED WITH TESTER RAILS
American 1790-1800 (Mahogany—Tester rails of pine)
NOW IN THE METROPOLITAN MUSEUM OF ART

FIELD BEDSTEAD
American Third Quarter XVIII Century

AN EXAMPLE fairly typical of the more simple highpost bedstead, as executed in colonial America, is that shown here.

The four posts, which are very slender and tapering, are turned, and depend mainly upon fluting and reeding for ornamentation. The shaft rests upon a turned base of classical profile and a ring breaks the long lines of the flutings about two-thirds of the way up. The capital is also turned with a double ring moulding and a plain tapered shaft extends to the framework above. The head posts, which, according to custom, are without decoration, are square and tapered with corners chamfered to such an extent that these posts become octagonal in section. Topping each post is an urn-shaped finial, delicately modeled. The two front legs are of the cabriole type terminating in bird's claw and ball feet.

An outstanding feature of this bedstead is the field top. The tester is cut in a serpentine curve whose center rises high above the horizontal members connecting the four posts. A solitary rod braces the tester at its peak.

It was the vogue to cover the tester frame with draperies which were finished along the horizontal framework and above the capitals of the foot posts with a valance. The back posts, as well as the space between them and the bed rails, were likewise covered with draped materials.

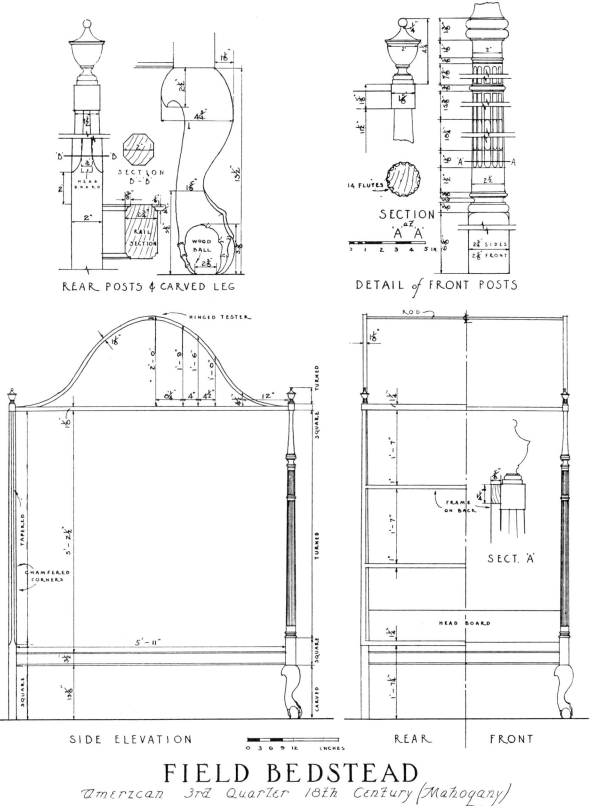

REAR POSTS & CARVED LEG

DETAIL of FRONT POSTS

SECTION D-D

HEAD BOARD

RAIL SECTION

WOOD BALL

SECTION A-A

14 FLUTES

0 1 2 3 4 5 IN.

2⅜ SIDES
2⅜ FRONT

HINGED TESTER

ROD

TURNED

SQUARE

TURNED

SQUARE

CARVED

TAPERED

CHAMFERED CORNERS

5'-2½"

5'-11"

SQUARE

FRAME ON BACK

SECT. A

HEAD BOARD

SIDE ELEVATION

0 3 6 9 12 INCHES

REAR | FRONT

FIELD BEDSTEAD
American 3rd Quarter 18th Century (Mahogany)

NOW IN THE MUSEUM OF RHODE ISLAND SCHOOL OF DESIGN

LOUIS XVI BEDSTEAD
XVIII Century

CONTEMPORANEOUS with the 18th century classical revival in England, ushered in by the brothers Adam, was a like revival in France, similar, except for minor variations inspired by the warmer tone of the Gallic tradition and conception. The furniture designed during the reign of Louis XVI is a direct outgrowth of this revival.

The elaborate and ornate patterns of the preceding years, with their baroque and rococo detail, were abandoned for more restrained classic lines and mouldings. The construction became rectilinear, lighter and more graceful, with pronounced architectural feeling. The swell and curve were not dispensed with but used with greater restraint.

The bed, shown on these pages, is of this period.

The delicate fabric, which composes the body of the head and foot frames, is characteristically used. Various types of satins and brocades were most frequently employed as upholstery.

The entire framework is handsomely carved with a diversity of motifs, all of classic derivation. Rarely were the frames left in their natural finish, but were painted and gilded, as is this example, to better harmonize with the painted interiors of the rooms then in vogue.

The air of ceremonious elegance, combined with a spirit of exuberance, employed with such distinction in Louis Seize furniture, met with the approval of the great English masters of design, Hepplewhite, Sheraton and the brothers Adam.

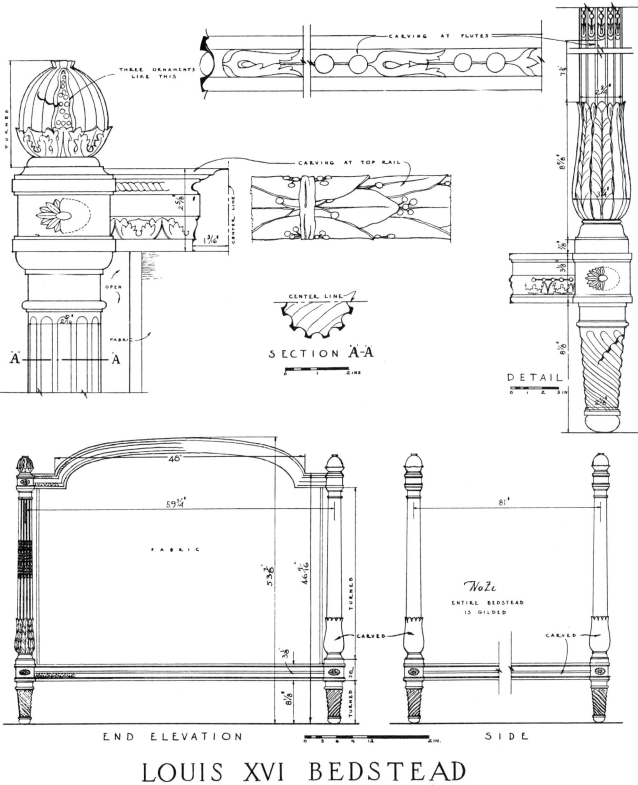

CARVING AT FLUTES

THREE ORNAMENTS
LIKE THIS

CARVING AT TOP RAIL

TURNED

2 5/8"

CENTER LINE

1 3/6"

OPEN

2 9/16"

FABRIC

A —— A

CENTER LINE

SECTION A-A

0   1   2 INS

7 1/4"

3/4"

8 5/8"

3/4"

7 7/8"

3/8"

8 1/8"

DETAIL

0 1 2 3 IN.

2 1/2"

48"

59 3/4"

FABRIC

53 1/2"

46 9/16"

TURNED

3 1/2"

CARVED

8 1/8"

TURNED SQ.

81"

Note
ENTIRE BEDSTEAD
IS GILDED

CARVED

END ELEVATION

0 3 6 9 12   2 IN.

SIDE

LOUIS XVI BEDSTEAD
18th Century (Beech ~ Gilded)
NOW IN THE BOSTON MUSEUM OF FINE ARTS

KNIFE BOX, STYLE OF HEPPLEWHITE
English 1775-1800

ON THE sideboards or side tables of the 18th century frequently stood knife boxes, usually in pairs. Toward the close of the century, the urn or vase shaped case was introduced and presented an opportunity for classic designing. Hepplewhite excelled in the execution of these accessories. Very frequently these boxes stood upon pedestals, which supplied storage space or were used as cellerettes or again as plate warmers.

As in the accompanying box, the knife holes were frequently arranged in rows forming concentric circles, into which the knives were placed with handles projecting. The lid was secured in place by a stem attached to the center of the box proper and provided with a spring to hold, when required, the lid in a raised position.

This urn, which closely follows prototypes made by Hepplewhite, rests upon a square base supported upon short bracket feet.

Inlay of vertical lines of stringing gave added grace to the classic shaping of the vase, while this same inlaid treatment is applied to the stepped divisions holding the knives and also to the stand and to the bracketed feet.

These cases were generally made of mahogany, satinwood or rosewood, or, again, were fashioned of painted wood.

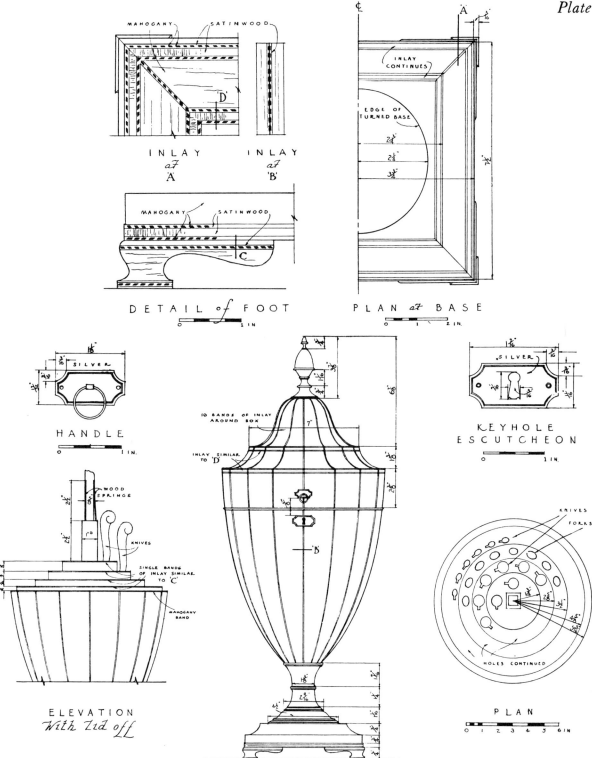

MAHOGANY   SATINWOOD

INLAY
at
'A'

INLAY
at
'B'

MAHOGANY   SATINWOOD

DETAIL of FOOT

0 · · · 1 IN.

C̄

A

INLAY
CONTINUES

EDGE OF
TURNED BASE

PLAN at BASE

0 · 1 · 2 IN.

SILVER

HANDLE

0 · · · 1 IN.

SILVER

KEYHOLE
ESCUTCHEON

0 · · · 1 IN.

WOOD
SPRINGS

KNIVES

SINGLE BAND
OF INLAY SIMILAR
TO 'C'

MAHOGANY
BAND

ELEVATION
With Lid off

10 BANDS OF INLAY
AROUND BOX

7"

INLAY SIMILAR
TO 'D'

'B'

KNIVES

FORKS

HOLES CONTINUED

PLAN

0 1 2 3 4 5 6 IN.

KNIFE BOX *Style of* HEPPLEWHITE
English 1775 – 1800 (Mahogany)
NOW IN THE MUSEUM OF RHODE ISLAND SCHOOL OF DESIGN

DRESSING GLASS

English 1790-1800

DRESSING glasses, mounted upon a box stand, came into vogue at the beginning of the 18th century. The stand was usually a small reproduction of the bureau upon which it stood. Hepplewhite has often been accredited with originating the oval and the shield shaped dressing glass. These shapes were in use before his influence was felt, although the weight of his authority was necessary to definitely establish their position.

An extremely ornate example is that illustrated here. It forms decorative adjunct to the handsome bow-front commode, illustrated on Plate 75, on which it was intended to rest. These elaborate mirrors afforded proper settings for their fair patrons, who were accustomed to receive visitors of both sexes while their elaborate coiffures were being arranged.

The broad alternating bands of dark and light wood, on the front of the box and those radiating at the top from the handsome shell motif, so frequently found on pieces of Hepplewhite design, are of the same general decorative scheme as the commode mentioned above. The brass mountings represent lions' masks and recall those placed on the large drawers of the commode.

The mirror frame, with its rich cresting and elaborate supports, is extravagantly carved and richly gilded.

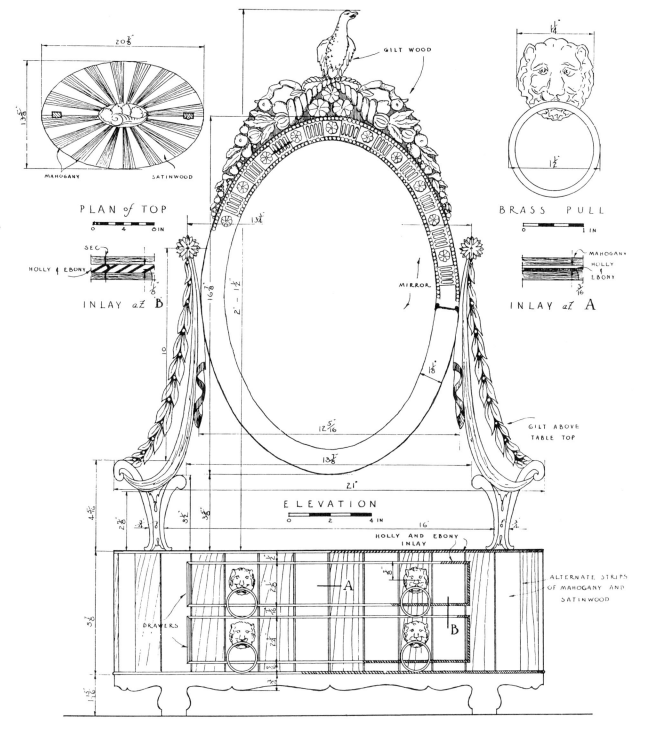

20⅝

13⅜

MAHOGANY   SATINWOOD

PLAN of TOP

0   4   8 IN

SEC

HOLLY & EBONY

INLAY at B

GILT WOOD

13¼

16⅝

2' - 1½

MIRROR

1⅛

12 5/16

13⅞

21

ELEVATION

0   2   4 IN

HOLLY AND EBONY
INLAY

16

GILT ABOVE
TABLE TOP

1¼

1½

BRASS PULL

0   1 IN

MAHOGANY
HOLLY
EBONY

3/16

INLAY at A

ALTERNATE STRIPS
OF MAHOGANY AND
SATINWOOD

A

B

DRAWERS

4 5/16

2⅜   3¼   3½   3⅜

3⅞

1 15/16

DRESSING ~ GLASS

English 1790 ~ 1800 (Mahogany and Satinwood)

NOW IN THE BOSTON MUSEUM OF FINE ARTS

MIRROR

American 1725-1750

IN KEEPING with the rich character of furniture produced in the first half of the 18th century is this American made mirror. At this time, the rococo spirit predominated, which is here adopted in the scrolled outlines and in the florid gilt ornament at the upper and lower portions of the frame. The combination of foliage motifs and the much favored C-scroll dominate this carved relief, whose major elements are in places perforated.

The frame is of the cut-work type, executed of mahogany veneer. The cresting and base are shaped and scrolled, producing an outline composed mainly of cyma curves, which at the top are connected by a hooped heading. The intricate scrolling of both top and bottom frames depicts a mastery of opposing curves.

Immediately surrounding the glass is a carved and gilded moulding of splayed form. The use of gilt with mahogany surfaces was frequently recommended by Chippendale, under whose regime this mirror was fashioned.

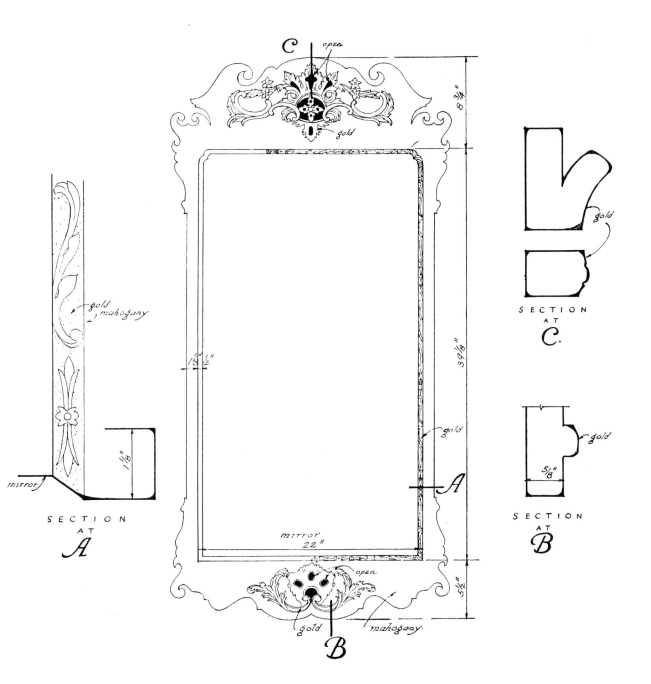

MIRROR
American 1725-1750 (Mahogany Veneer)
NOW IN THE METROPOLITAN MUSEUM OF ART

FIRE-SCREEN
American 1750-1780

THIS very fine example of Pole-screen was made in America when Thomas Chippendale was turning out his best tripod tables and firescreens in England. The ancient form of the tripod was adapted to modern uses and carried to its greatest excellence by this master. In this American-made piece of furniture are many of the most characteristic features of the Chippendale style, such as the bulbous but delicate turnings at the base of the pole, and the graceful legs with claws and feet gripping the ball. The shaft base is carved with spiral beadings and shell pattern and a well designed finial terminates the pole.

The rectangular screen consists of a frame on which needlepoint is stretched on the outer side and on the inside a geometrical patchwork made of satin, silks and velvets. The sliding frame is guided at the bottom by a metal ring and is held in place by a wide brass band at the top, equipped with screw and button.

This fire-screen was executed in mahogany, as were most of the fine small pieces of the Chippendale period, the strength of this wood lending itself to these slender and delicate contours.

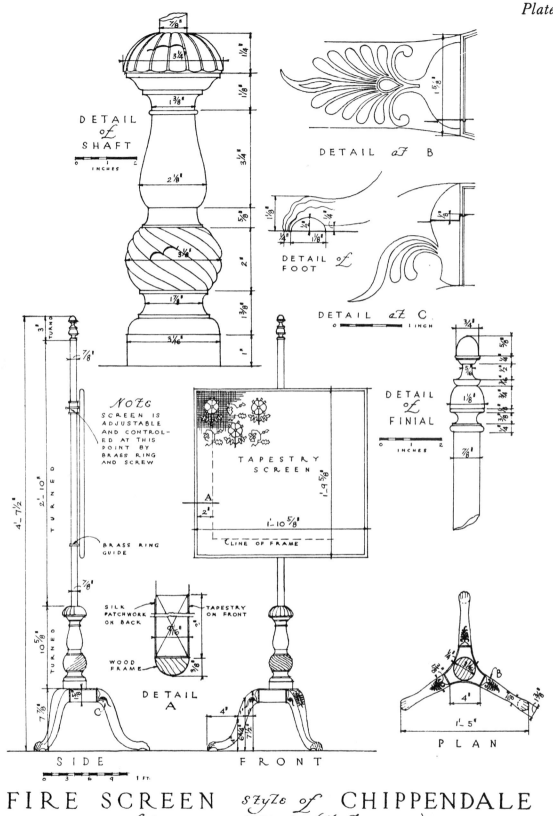

DETAIL of SHAFT

DETAIL of B

DETAIL of FOOT

DETAIL of C

DETAIL of FINIAL

NOTE
SCREEN IS
ADJUSTABLE
AND CONTROL-
ED AT THIS
POINT BY
BRASS RING
AND SCREW

TAPESTRY
SCREEN

BRASS RING
GUIDE

SILK
PATCHWORK
ON BACK

TAPESTRY
ON FRONT

WOOD
FRAME

DETAIL A

LINE OF FRAME

SIDE

FRONT

PLAN

FIRE SCREEN *Style of* CHIPPENDALE
American 1750-80 (Mahogany)
NOW IN THE METROPOLITAN MUSEUM OF ART

MINIATURE TALL CLOCK
American 1730-1749

IN THE last years of the 17th century the tall clock was imported to New England, and from that time their local manufacture became popular in the Colonies. Among the many excellent clock makers of this time, and the one to whom the mahogany bonnet-top clock shown is attributed, was Thomas Claggett of Newport, R. I.

It was the fashion of this time to make miniature or bijou cased clocks along the lines of the taller clocks and with works of brass. These were often called "Grandmother Clocks." The example shown follows this fashion, standing approximately five feet high.

A common feature of the 18th century tall clock is the scroll top and the broken arch surmounted with wooden balls. In this particular case the inner ends of the scrolls are finished with turned rosettes and the wooden balls have the upper half carved and are surmounted with a delicately carved finial of spiral flame-like pattern. The fluted columns at the corners of the hood case are of Chippendale inspiration.

Mahogany as a fashionable wood was introduced a few years previous to the execution of this clock and is the wood used in this example.

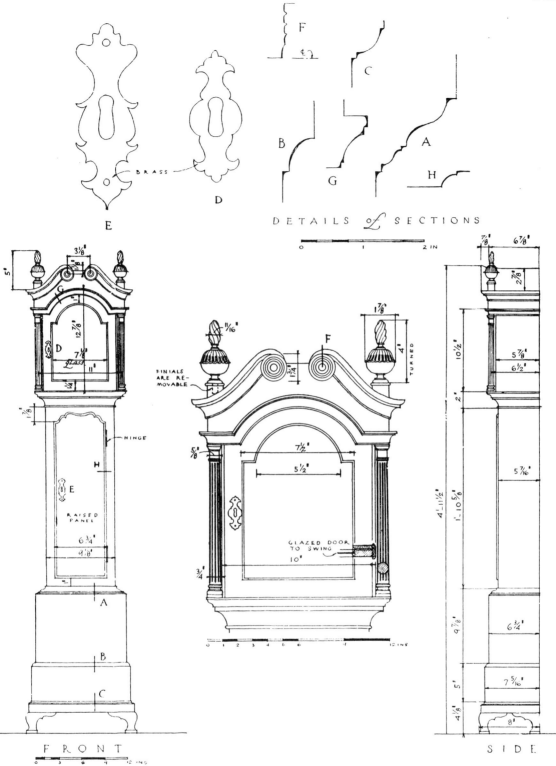

DETAILS *of* SECTIONS

BRASS

E   D

FRONT

FINIALS ARE RE-MOVABLE

GLAZED DOOR TO SWING

RAISED PANEL

HINGE

SIDE

TURNED

MINIATURE TALL CLOCK
American 1730-1749 (Mahogany)
NOW IN THE METROPOLITAN MUSEUM OF ART

A BIBLIOGRAPHY OF BOOKS ON FURNITURE
CONTAINING MEASURED DRAWINGS

1. *General Works*

English decoration and furniture from 1500-1820. 1. English decoration and furniture during the Tudor, Elizabethan and early Stuart periods (1500-1660), by M. Jourdain. 2. Decoration in England from 1660-1770, by Francis Lenygon. 3. Furniture in England from 1660-1760, by Francis Lenygon. 4. English decoration and furniture of the later XVIIIth and early XIXth centuries (1760-1820), by M. Jourdain. London, Batsford, 1922-1924.

A monumental work. Only occasional measured drawings, taken from older sources, but highly useful in their selection and context.

Dumonthier, Ernest.

Les plus beaux meubles des ministères et administrations publiques. Lits et lits de repos. Paris, Éditions Albert Morancé. [192—]   44 plates.

Photographs of beds, sofas and chairs with scales drawn in.

Marshall, Arthur.

Specimens of antique carved furniture and woodwork . . . London, Allen, 1888.   50 plates.

A Victorian reproduction of 15th-18th century pieces, with the emphasis on the earlier phases.

Paris. Musées du Louvre et de Cluny.

Collection de meubles anciens, relevés, d'après les originaux, a l'échelle de 10 centimètres pour mètre, par Ch. Ruprich, architecte, et dessinés par E. Bajot, architecte d'ameublement . . . Paris, André, Daly fils et cie, 1890. 50 plates.

Particularly important for the 15th and 16th centuries.

Prignot, Eugène.

L'ameublement moderne, par Prignot. Liénard, Coignet et plusieurs autres artistes spéciaux. Paris, C. Claesen [1880]   2 vols.

English and French furniture from late Medieval through Louis XVI.

Townsend, W. G. Paulson.

Measured drawings of French furniture from the collection in South Kensington Museum. London and New York, Truslove, Hanson and Comba, 1899.   121 plates.

From the late 15th through the 18th century.

Warne, E. J.

Furniture mouldings from 1574 to 1820 . . . London, Ernest Benn, 1923. 140 plates.

2. *Eighteenth century French*

Hessling, Egon.

Le mobilier Louis XV au Musée du Louvre. Paris, Librairie Hessling, 1910.   28 plates, 9 with measured drawings.

Lalonde, Richard de.

Recueil des oeuvres de Richard de Lalonde, dessinateur et décorateur (époque Louis XVI) . . . Paris, Rouveyre [1889]   113 plates.

3. *Eighteenth century English*

Adam, Robert and James.

The works in architecture . . . London, Aux dépens des auteurs, 1778-1786.   3 vols. (107 plates) . 3rd vol. 1822.

No furniture designs, but priceless measured details and ornaments, especially ceilings and moldings. Reprinted by Thézard fils, Dourdan, 1902.

Chippendale, Thomas.

The gentleman and cabinet-maker's director. Being a large collection of . . . designs of household furniture in the Gothic, Chinese and modern taste . . . London, The Author, 1754.   161 plates.

The primary source book for all later Chippendale design. The third edition (1762, 200 plates) is to be reprinted by Dover Publications, Inc., in 1965.

Chippendale, Thomas.

Chippendale's ornaments and interior decorations in the old French styles . . . London, John Weale [1858-59]   32 plates.

Drawn and engraved by M. Lock. Mostly frames, stands, watch cases, brackets, etc. Only a few scales are given.

Heaton, John Aldam.

Furniture and decoration in England during the eighteenth century. Facsimile reproductions of the choicest examples from the works of Chippendale, Adam, Richardson, Hepplewhite [*sic*], Sheraton, Pergolesi and others . . . London, Bumpus, 1889.   2 vols. (200 plates) .

Hepplewhite A. and Co.

The cabinet-maker and upholsterer's guide; or, repository of designs for every article of household furniture . . . with a scale to each, and an explanation in letter press. London, Taylor, 1787.   124 plates.

The primary source book for all later Hepplewhite design. Reprinted by Towse publishing company in New York, 1942. The third edition, 1794, reprinted by Batsford, London, 1897.

Household furniture in genteel taste for the year 1760, by a society of upholsterers, cabinet-makers, etc. . . . London, Robert Sayer [1760] 60 plates.

Ince, William and Mayhew, John.

The universal system of household furniture. London, c.1762.   95 engraved plates of 300 designs.

Sheraton, Thomas.

The cabinet-maker and upholsterer's drawing book . . . London, Bensley, 1794. 2nd edition.   60 plates and an appendix.

The whole range of decoration and ornamental details as well as furniture design.

Swan, Abraham.

The British architect; or, the builders treasury of staircases . . . London, Robert Sayer [1758]   60 plates.

Staircases, arches, doors and windows, chimney-pieces, decorations, etc. Reprinted in Philadelphia by John Norman in 1775 and extensively used by Colonial designers.

4. *Early American*

Benjamin, Asher.

The country builder's assistant . . . Illus. with new and useful designs of frontispieces, chimney pieces, etc. . . . . Greenfield, Mass. T. Dickman, 1797. 30 plates.

A primary source of early American design. Reprinted in many editions.

French, Leigh Jr.

Colonial interiors. Photographs and measured drawings of the colonial and early federal periods. New York, Helburn, 1923.   125 plates.

Plates 107-124 contain measured drawings of panels and moldings.

Goforth, W. Davenport, and McAuley, William J.

Old colonial architectural details in and around Philadelphia. 50 plates of scaled and measured drawings. New York, Helburn, 1890.

Useful for gates, newel posts, fan lights, moldings, mantles, etc.

Margon, Lester.

Construction of American furniture treasures . . . New York,, The Home craftsman publishing corporation, 1949.   38 plates, 344 detail drawings.

"The work of the most famous early American cabinet makers."

Millar, Donald.

Colonial furniture . . . New York, Architectural book publishing company, 1925.   31 plates.

Mill· r, Donald.

Measured drawings of some colonial and Georgian houses. New York, Architectural book publishing company, 1930.   3 vols.

Panels, moldings, doors, windows, stairs, mantles, etc.

Nye, Alvan Crocker.

A collection of scale drawings, details, and sketches of what is commonly known as colonial furniture . . . New York, Helburn, 1895.   55 plates.

The monograph series recording the architecture of the American colonies and the early republic. New York, Whitehead, 1915-1940. 26 vols.

Also called the White pine series. No furniture, but numerous ornamental details.

Sims, Joseph P., and Willing, Charles.

Old Philadelphia colonial details. New York, Architectural book publishing company, 1914.   55 plates.

Panels, mantles, railings, doors, stairways.

Wallis, Frank E.

American architecture, decoration and furniture of the eighteenth century . . . New York, Wenzel [1896]   52 plates.

"A collection of measured drawings and sketches of existing work, with an addition of modern work of the same period."

Wallis, Frank E.

Old colonial architecture and furniture . . . Boston, Polley and company, 1887.   60 plates.

Ware, William R.

The Georgian period, being photographs and measured drawings of colonial work with text. New York, U. P. C. book publishing company, 1923.   6 parts (454 plates).

Useful for its many details: cornices, moldings, panels, stairs, church pews, pulpits, etc.

5. *Empire and Regency*

Bridgens, Richard.

Designs for Grecian and other furniture, candelabra, and interior decorations. London [published in conjunction with H. Shaw] 1838.   60 plates.

Hall, John.

The cabinet maker's assistant . . . Baltimore, John Murphy, 1840.   44 plates.

Reprinted by National Superior Inc., New York, 1944.

Hope, Thomas.

Household furniture and interior decoration. London, Tiranti, 1946.   60 plates.

Reprint of the 1807 edition.

King, Thomas.

The modern style of cabinet work exemplified . . . London, the author, 1829.   72 plates.

Percier, Charles and Fontaine, Pierre François Léonard.

Recueil de décorations intérieures, comprenant tout ce qui a rapport à l'ameublement. Paris, Didot, 1812.   72 plates.

A great variety of French Empire design, but not measured throughout.

Santi,

Modèles de meubles et de décorations intérieures pour l'ameublement, tels que tables, secrétaires, commodes, bureaux, miroirs . . . Paris, Bance, 1828.   74 plates.

Schinkel, Karl Friedrich.

Sammlung von möbel-entwürfen . . . Potsdam, Riegel, 1852.   16 plates,
Representative of German design.

Smith, George.

The cabinet-maker and upholsterer's guide: being a complete drawing book . . . for household furniture, and interior decoration . . . London, Jones, 1826.   145 plates.

One of the most important books for the taste of the 1820's.

Smith, George.

A collection of designs for household furniture and interior decoration . . . London, Taylor, 1808.   158 plates.

Taylor, John.

Original and novel designs for decorative household furniture, more particularly for the department connected with upholstery . . . London, the author, 1824.   30 plates.

6. *Victorian*

Entwürfe zu möbeln. Cassel, 1851.   40 plates.

Mostly Gothic revival.

Mennel, Thomas.

Wiener vorlagen für möbel-tischlerei. Vienna, Schroll, 1892.   24 plates.

Viennese 19th century designs.

Paukert, Franz.

Die zimmergotik in Deutsch-Tirol. Leipzig, Seemann, 1892.   4 parts (128 plates).

Peasant-derived neo-gothic furniture, decoration and ornament from Tirol.

Schaupert, Karl.

Entwürfe in bürgerlicher ausstattung zu den hauptsächlichsten möbeln . . . Weimar, Voigt, 1881.   25 plates.

Schwenke, F.

Ausgeführte möbel und zimmereinrichtungen der gegenwart . . . Berlin, Wasmuth, 1881.   2 vols. (144 plates).

Representative of Victorian design in the Germany of the 1880's.

Talbert, B. J.

Gothic forms applied to furniture, metal work and decoration for domestic purposes . . . Boston, Osgood, 1873.   30 plates.

Printed in America from an English source.

7. *Modern*

Boltenstern, Erich.

Wiener möbel . . . Stuttgart, Hoffmann, 1935. 96 pages of illustrations.

Fabbro, Mario dal.

Modern furniture, its design and construction. New York, Reinhold publishing company, 1949.   159 pages of illustrations, 16 pages appendix.

Hooper, John and Rodney.

Modern furniture and fittings . . . London, New York, Batsford, 1948. 21 double-page drawings.

Hooper, Rodney.

Modern furniture making and design. Peoria, Ill., Manual arts press, 1939.

Measured illustrations in text. First published in England under the title "Woodcraft in design and practice."

Simons, William L.

Furniture for to-day and to-morrow, with details, scale drawings and pen and ink sketches . . . New York, Architectural book publishing company, 1928.   80 plates.